THE SAILING
POCKET COMPANION

Miles Kendall

PAVILION

A Think Book for Pavilion Books

This edition published by Pavilion Books in 2008
First published in the United Kingdom in 2004 by Robson Books
10 Southcombe Street, London W14 0RA

Imprints of Anova Books Company Ltd

Text and design © Think Publishing 2004
The moral rights of the authors have been asserted

Edited by Miles Kendall
The Companion team: Tilly Boulter, James Collins, Rhiannon Guy,
Emma Jones, Jo Swinnerton, Lou Millward Tait, Malcolm Tait
and Marcus Trower

Think Publishing
The Pall Mall Deposit
124–128 Barlby Road, London W10 6BL
www.thinkpublishing.co.uk

ISBN 978-1-862057-96-8

2 4 6 8 10 9 7 5 3 1

Printed and bound by Millenium International Printing, China

www.anovabooks.com

THE POCKET COMPANION SERIES:
COLLECT THEM ALL

INTRODUCTION

There is a magic to the sea. It draws us to it and holds us in its thrall. We want to make our homes beside it, swim in it, holiday by it shores. It is a living thing, never still. Its mood can change from calm and peaceful to violent and deadly within minutes. It can erode headlands or give birth to new islands. And to venture out to sea under sail is the greatest thrill of all.

The romance of sailing is undeniable. Gliding through the water, the wind in your hair and the sun on your face is as good as it gets – though it isn't always so blissful. When there's a gale blowing and your crewmates are bent over the side, bidding farewell to their lunch, things may not seem so rosy. But that's the beauty of going to sea – you never know quite what to expect. There is always a new lesson to be learnt or a new delight to be experienced.

There are plenty of publications that explain how to sail – but this is not one of them. Instead it is an eclectic collection of nautical knowledge. It seeks to cast some light on why people cast off their lines and set course for somewhere beyond the horizon. I hope that it will also remind us that sailing is something that shouldn't be taken too seriously. There exists a great body of writing on sailing – this is just a drop in the ocean.

Miles Kendall, Editor

DOING ANYTHING NICE FOR
YOUR HOLIDAYS?

Fancy a week away from it all on a yacht? What about soaking up the Mediterranean sunshine or escaping the European winter for rum and fun in the Caribbean? In that case, why not charter *Mirabella V*, the largest single-masted yacht in the world.

Launched in 2004, *Mirabella V* is an awe-inspiring 246ft 8in long and almost 50ft wide. Her masts stands 292ft high, which prevents her from passing under the Golden Gate Bridge. A massive hydraulic lifting ram can raise the keel from 33ft to a mere 13ft.

Owner Joe Vittoria made his fortune when he sold the Avis car rental empire but still needs to charter her out to cover the bills and $50 million building costs. The $350,000 weekly rate may seem steep, but that's not the end of it. 'Parking' *Mirabella V* for the night can set you back about $2,000 – and then there's the pilot's fees, food, drinks and fuel. A 10% tip is considered the minimum, meaning that the bill for your week in the sun is likely to exceed $335,000.

So what do you get for your money? A 600-bottle wine cellar, two swimming pools (one fresh water, one salt) and a crew of 11, but only 12 berths for you and your friends. Book now to avoid disappointment.

COOKING FAT

You don't have to spend too long wandering around a marina before coming across a catamaran with the name *Cooking Fat* inscribed proudly across her sterns. A strange name for a boat, you may think – until you transpose the initial letters.

THE REALITY OF SAILING

Smells

Take six people who can only bring limited changes of clothes on board and place them in the close confines of a yacht. Make them wear thick clothing and rubber boots. Add regular physical exercise to work up a sweat. Ensure the limited supply of water combined with the cramped confines of the heads or shower make them unwilling to wash.

Prevent any airflow through the cabin by keeping hatches closed in case waves break over the boat. Feed them on bacon butties, beer and curry. Install a tiny toilet with yards of piping in which pongs can fester. It's no wonder that yachtsmen head for the showers before the bar after a few days at sea.

CHARTING THE HEIGHTS

You can't find just any old building on an Admiralty chart. Only the following can become annotated landmarks:

Brick kiln	Institute	Refinery
Castle	Lattice tower	Sailor's home
Cathedral	Lookout station	School
Cement works	Machine house	Sewage works
Cold store	Mast	Spa hotel
Column	Monastery, Convent	Structure
Electric works	Mooring mast	Telegraph office
Factory	Multi-storey building	Town hall
Floodlight	Naval college	Warehouse
Gas works	Navigation school	Water mill
Greenhouse	Office	Water works
Hotel	Observatory	Well
House	Power station	
Hut	Pyramid	

SAILING TERMS THAT
CONFUSE LANDLUBBERS

Weigh anchor

Anchors are, by and large, fairly heavy. It is one of their great assets when it comes to stopping a boat from drifting away. One's choice of anchor is dictated by two things: weight and design. There is a bewildering range of designs now available.

In the olden days anchors looked like the ones you still occasionally see on tattoos, but that has all changed. You can now have a plough, a fortress or a Danforth at the end of your chain – and they all come in a variety of weights. However if asked to 'weigh anchor' you should refrain from getting the scales out. You are being requested to pull the anchor up from the seabed – though you will get a fair idea of how much it weighs in the process.

A NAUTICAL STORY

This true story recently appeared as a reader's confession in the pages of *Yachting Monthly*.

A family go for a sail on their yacht. They anchor off a remote beach and go ashore to explore. Mum and Dad climb through waist-high heather to the clifftop while their two boys play on the sand. On reaching the top, the parents see that the bigger of the boys has his brother on the ground and is pushing sand into his face. 'Stop that at once!' shouts the father, at which point a young couple emerge shocked and in a state of undress from the heather just a few yards from where the parents stand. Thinking that the order had been directed at them, the lovers hastily button themselves up while the parents, equally embarrassed, mutter an apology and head back to the beach as quickly as they can.

THINGS THAT GO MOO IN THE NIGHT

Night watches can be long and lonely affairs. It is easy for your mind to wander when you're huddled in the cockpit with one eye on the compass and one scanning the horizon for other ships. Many yachtsmen experience nocturnal visitors of different shapes and sizes. Some hear strange animal sounds – cats, dogs, pigs and even cows – others recognise human voices among the gurgle of the wake and whistle of the rigging.

Seafarers also talk of seeing strange things at night. Some are just illusions – a coiled rope becomes a sleeping snake; others actually hallucinate and see things that are not there at all. Joshua Slocum, the pioneering US yachtsman, told of someone coming aboard his yacht at sea and taking the helm for several hours. Visitors have been seen standing at the bow and even on top of the mast. Indeed a study in 1972 found that half the sailors who had crossed the Atlantic single-handed had experienced some type of hallucination. Sleeplessness, solitude and stress are the likely causes – though some still blame the mermaids.

TO THE MED THE EASY WAY

If you want to cruise the Med but don't fancy sailing out into the Atlantic and across the Bay of Biscay then why not meander through French rivers and canals? Starting from Le Havre the route is:

River Seine
River Yonne
Canal de Bourgogne
Tunnel to Dijon
River Saône
River Rhône
The Mediterranean

It is not just the surface of the sea that is always moving – its level is constantly changing too. Depths of water and the heights of rocks and sandbanks on a chart are measured from a common level of tide known as the chart datum. This is also referred to as the Lowest Astronomical Tide as it is the lowest level to which the tide will fall due to any combination of astronomical conditions. It is very rare for the tide to ever drop this low, but cartographers are a naturally cautious lot.

Look at the areas of water on a chart and you will see a lot of numbers. These are depths or heights in metres and tenths of metres. An underlined number indicates a drying height of a feature that can be covered and uncovered by the tide. Thus an underlined number three shows an area of seabed that stands three metres above the level of chart datum. Were the number three not under-lined, you would know that at this spot the sea was three metres deeper than the level of chart datum.

Tides are all added to chart datum. If there is a four-metre tide, our three-metre rock will be a metre beneath the waves, while there will now be seven metres of water at the point that was three metres deep.

Tides are never constant and this complicates things even more. Spring tides are big tides: the water rises and falls more than average. These are the tides that reveal rarely seen wrecks and sandbanks. Neap tides are altogether more modest, rising and falling less than average.

A ready reckoning system helps sailors make sense of all this tidal trickery. Average heights of tide for both neaps and springs are given, so that you know what to expect. Mean High Water Springs (MHWS) is the average height of the highest high tides and is important to know, as it is the level from which the chartered heights of objects on land are measured. If a chart says that a lighthouse is 30 metres high, you know that it is 30 metres above MHWS. This is useful, as knowing how high an object is allows you to calculate how far you are from it.

Establishing what sort of tide, or height, or depth is being referred to can be a confusing process, yet it is child's play compared to actually working out how much water you will have under your keel at a certain place at a certain time. It is principally for this reason that many sailors have such a soft spot for the virtually tideless Mediterranean.

THOSE SEVEN SEAS IN FULL

Useful for people who like pub quizzes.
Second only to being able to name all seven dwarfs.

Arctic
Antarctic
North Atlantic
South Atlantic
Indian
North Pacific
South Pacific

NAUTICAL PUZZLES

An impoverished yachtsman arrives at a fuel pontoon with a five-litre container and asks the attendant to put four litres of diesel into it. Unfortunately, the pump is broken and the only measure the fuel man has is a three-litre jug. How can the men measure out exactly four litres of diesel using just these two containers?

Answer on page 145

RULE BRITANNIA!

Yacht racing became the sport of kings when, at the end of the nineteenth century, the royalty of Europe commissioned a series of stunning yachts in which to compete against each other. Most famous in home waters was *Britannia*, which was built for the Prince of Wales, later to become King Edward VII. Edward's nephew, Kaiser Wilhelm II, had bought a yacht of his own the previous year, and following *Britannia*'s launch, he upgraded to the majestic cutter, *Meteor*.

Britannia was a spectacular vessel, some 102ft long with a 110ft mast and 10,000 square-foot sail. It took more than a dozen men to hoist her mainsail. And she could sail. With a deep keel and powerful rig she was the fastest boat on the water and saw off competition from Europe and America. What's more, by taking the lion's share of silverware she prompted yacht clubs, designers and fellow competitors to rethink regulations governing the design of yachts to create a more level playing field.

PEES AT SEA

Toilets on boats – or heads, as they are properly called – are generally cramped and often malodorous affairs. If the vessel is heeled over or pitching through the waves, one is likely to emerge relieved but battered. How much nicer to let it all hang out in the open air and top up the sea directly – and that is what most yachtsmen do when away from the crowds. Such *al fresco* urination is not without its risks. Standing on the gunwhale, leaning overboard, one hand for the boat and one for the old chap, you put yourself in a precarious position. Many a sailor's corpse has been dragged from the water with the fly undone. So if you do pee at sea, make sure you hold on tight, and always have your back to the wind.

TALES FROM THE OCEAN

*Jonah thanked the whale and sat down with a sigh.
He was glad to be alive but aware he smelled strongly
of plankton.*

TYPHOON WARNING

The Royal Hong Kong Yacht Club occupies a stunning site on the edge of one of the world's most famous harbours. The club has not moved its location, but anyone who visited it in the first half of last century would not recognise it now. The reason is that the club was originally built on an island and sailors would take small local boats, sampans, out to it. However, as Hong Kong prospered, land became a costly commodity and massive land reclamation projects were carried out to provide more land for skyscrapers. Eventually Hong Kong's expanding shoreline reached the island and the sampan owners were out of a job.

They were not the only ones to regret the island's absorption. When typhoon warnings were issued in the past there would be a rush of yachtsmen out to the island, safe in the knowledge that within hours they would be trapped there, perhaps for days, with nothing to do but sit in the bar and get drunk.

SAINTS FOR SEAFARERS

If you're in peril on the sea and no one else can help you, you could try calling on the help of one of the many and varied patron saints of seafarers, sailors, mariners, boatmen and watermen.

Saint	Memorial day
Anthony of Padua	13 June
Barbara	4 December
Botulph	17 June
Brendan the Navigator	16 May
Brigid of Ireland	1 February
Christina of Bolsena	24 July
Christopher	25 July
Clement I	23 November
Cuthbert	20 March
Erasmus	2 June
Eulalia	12 February
Francis of Paola	2 April
Jodocus	13 December
John Roche	30 August
Julian the Hospitaller	12 February
Michael the Archangel	29 September
Nicholas of Myra	6 December
Nicholas of Tolentino	10 September
Our Lady, Star of the Sea	Multiple days
Our Lady of Mount Carmel	16 July
Peter Gonzales	14 April
Phocas the Gardener	23 July
Walburga	25 February

NAUTICAL PUZZLES

Which racing yachtswoman owned a boat whose politically incorrect name might have put her in a sticky situation?
Answer on page 145

BLACK STUFF AT THE BOAT SHOW

A curious thing happens to sailors at the annual London Boat Show. No matter what their tipple of choice is for the other 364 days of the year, everyone drinks Guinness. This strange phenomenon could be explained away if there were numerous young lovelies serving these old sea dogs their pints of stout, but nothing could be further from the truth. The same organised crew of middle-aged men are employed year after year to pull the pints, and pull them they do – some 57,000 a week. The Guinness stand is the universal rendezvous. If you turn up at the Boat Show alone, head here. Even if you've never been near a boat in your life you're bound to meet someone you know.

WHAT A BLAST

Different vessels make different sounds in fog

Type of boat and its sound signal
(normally at least every two minutes)
Boats under 12m, *loud sound*
Powered vessel moving, *one long*
Powered vessel stopped but not anchored, *two long*
Tug, *one long, two short*
Vessel being towed, *one long, three short*
Sailing vessel, *one long, two short*
Vessels restricted in ability to manoeuvre,
one long, two short
Trawler, *one long, two short*
Vessel aground, *three single strokes before
and after rapid ringing of the ship's bell*
Anchored vessel (less than 100m long),
rapid ringing of bell at least every minute
Anchored vessel (over 100m), *rapid ringing of bell,
followed by gong rung rapidly near stern*

CRUISING COCKTAILS

Sea breeze

Two types of sea breeze can be found at sea and both can serve the yachtsman well. The first occurs when the sun heats the land, causing the air above it to warm and rise. The cooler air over the sea is drawn onto the land to replace the heated air and an onshore sea breeze is created.

The second sort of sea breeze is also found on warm summer days but easier to create. Simply take two parts vodka, three parts cranberry juice and three parts grapefruit juice. Pour over ice into a highball glass. Garnish with a slice of lime. Recline in cockpit and enjoy.

DRAKE TIES THE KNOT

The point at which the homeward path of a round-the-world passage crosses the outward bound route is where a circumnavigator 'ties the knot' – and the first Englishman to do so was Sir Francis Drake. It is believed that Drake learned the ropes in the Thames coastal trade before going to sea properly, where he showed great aptitude and quickly rose up the ranks. In 1577 he was appointed to command the first English expedition to circumnavigate the globe. With five ships and some 160 men, he set sail on 13 December from Plymouth. The journey was full of incident, perhaps the most dramatic episode being the trial and beheading of Thomas Doughty, captain of one of the ships, on a charge of mutiny. Two of the smaller ships were sunk on purpose, another was separated from Drake's *Golden Hind* in a storm, and the remaining small sloop was lost at sea. Drake returned to England in 1580 and presented Queen Elizabeth with gold, silver and jewels taken from Spanish treasure ships he had raided off the Pacific Coast of Peru and Mexico.

FERRY NUFF

If you don't fancy hoisting sail yourself, you can always do it the easy way and get a ferry across the Channel. You'll be in good company, as legions of yachtsmen are now doing their bit for entente cordiale by keeping their boats in France and commuting to them, appropriately enough, by ferry.

From	To	Hours	Company
Plymouth	Santander	18	Brittany Ferries
Plymouth	Roscoff	6	Brittany Ferries
Poole	Cherbourg	4¼	Brittany Ferries
Poole	St Malo	6	Condor Ferries
Portsmouth	St Malo	9	Brittany Ferries
Portsmouth	Le Havre	5½	LD Lines
Portsmouth	Bilbao	35	P&O Ferries
Portsmouth	Cherbourg	4¾	Condor Ferries
Portsmouth	Cherbourg	3-5	Brittany Ferries
Portsmouth	Caen	3½	Brittany Ferries
Newhaven	Dieppe	5	Transmanche
Dover	Boulogne	1	Speed Ferries
Dover	Calais	1½	Sea France
Dover	Calais	1¼	P&O Ferries
Dover	Dunkirk	2	Norfolkline

NAUTICAL PUZZLES

You are sailing along when your yacht hits something in the water. There is a hole in the side of the boat over which you must secure a 28in by 28in wooden board. You'll need to secure the board with 29 nails on each side of the square. Each nail must be at the same distance from the neighbouring nails.
How many nails will you need?
Answer on page 145

SEA SAYINGS

As the crow flies

Crows are not sea birds and will head for land by the most direct route (as the crow flies). When unsure of their position in coastal waters, ships would release a caged crow. The crow would fly upwards until it spied land and then head for the shore, giving the vessel some sort of a navigational fix. The best place to follow the crow's progress was from a platform near the top of the mast – the crow's nest.

FOLKBOAT

She's old-fashioned and she's bang up-to-date. She's a gentleman's cruiser that is thrashed round the cans. She's a coastal potterer that has been sailed around the world.

The Folkboat is full of surprises and contradictions.

The result of a Scandinavian design competition, the Folkboat ended up being designed by committee after no one winner was selected. That was in 1941 and the first Folkboats came to the UK later that decade. It proved sea-kindly and exciting to race, and a class association was formed. Folkboats have been built in many countries and in many different ways since, and there are all sorts of variations on the Folkboat theme.

A NAUTICAL JOKE

A yachtsman is sailing along when the boom knocks him on the head and he falls overboard. When he comes round, he's on a beach. The sand is dark red. He can't believe it. The sky is dark red. He walks around a bit and sees that there is dark red grass, dark red birds and dark red fruit on the dark red trees. He's shocked when he finds that his skin is starting to turn dark red too.

'Oh no!' he cries, 'I've been marooned!'

SAILING FILMS

Capturing the might and majesty of the ocean is difficult when confined to a studio lot at Pinewood or Hollywood. Waves just don't look right when they are created to float a model boat in a special-effects tank, though computer-generated animation is a big leap forward. Some directors even film at sea. Here are a few of the best sailing films.

Message in a Bottle
A sentimental affair with Kevin Costner as the owner of a pretty wooden sloop.

The Thomas Crown Affair
Not about sailing at all but contains thrilling footage of a catamaran race that culminates in a spectacular capsize.

Wind
Matthew Modine is the America's Cup skipper battling for national pride. Lots of sailing footage compensates for the implausible story.

The Old Man and the Sea
Hemingway's classic tale of the sea, wonderfully done for the big screen. Nominated for Oscars for Best Cinematography and Best Actor, and won an Oscar for Best Score.

The Perfect Storm
Several boats are caught up in the vicious weather that decimates a North American fishing fleet. The stuff of nightmares.

The Riddle of the Sands
Michael York stars in this wonderfully dated adaptation of Erskine Childer's thriller. Great for lovers of wooden cruising yachts.

Master and Commander
Slow-paced swashbuckler for the twenty-first century. The storm scenes are the most convincing to ever grace the silver screen.

Waterworld
Ridiculous but watchable futuristic fable with Kevin Costner playing the seaman who starts to smell something fishy – himself.

THEY DON'T NAME THEM
LIKE THAT ANY MORE

Some Royal Navy ship names from the good old days

Indomitable (1907)
Inflexible (1907)
Invincible (1907; sunk 1916)
Superb (1907)
Indefatigable (1909; sunk 1916)
Thunderer (1911)
Audacious (1912)
Valiant (1914)
Courageous (1916)
Furious (1916)
Glorious (1916)
Renown (1916)
Repulse (1916; sunk 1941)

MEET THE FLEET

The following are the boats of the Royal National Lifeboat Institution's fleet. All of them are paid for purely by voluntary donations.

Class	Length (m)	Crew	Top speed (knots)
Severn	17	6	25
Trent	14.2	6	25
Arun	16	6	18
Tyne	14.3	6	17
Mersey	11.7	6	17
Tamar	16	6	25
B Class (Atlantic)	8.5	3	35
D Class	4.9	3	25
E Class	9	3	40
Hovercraft	8.1	3	30

HOW TO GET KNOTTED

The bowline

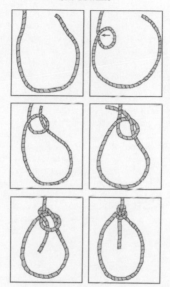

Take a long working end of a rope over the standing
part to form a small loop. Hold the loop in place with
one hand. Pass the working end through the loop from
back to front. Take the working end behind the
standing part. Now pass the working end up through
the loop from front to back. Pull on the standing part
and on the double working end to tighten the knot.
Alternatively: the rabbit goes up the hole, round the
tree and back down the hole.

THE COST OF A HONEYCOMB
SANDWICH

A strong boat used to mean a heavy boat, but the advent of new materials has made it possible to build boats that are both incredibly strong and light. Weight is kept to a minimum by combining an outer shell of a hard material with a filling of a lighter material. The technique is known as sandwich construction and glassfibre was first used as the bread and balsawood as the filling. When Kevlar and carbon composite materials became available to boat builders, a whole new world of interesting possibilities opened up.

By combining outer layers of Kevlar and carbon with a foam filling, an immensely strong sandwich can be created and many modern racing hulls are made from such materials. One of the strongest and lightest sandwiches available to the modern designer is the honeycomb sandwich: cells of hi-tech Nomex paper, looking just like honeycomb, stand between outer layers of woven Kevlar creating a light but rigid structure.

These modern space-age materials are prohibitively expensive for all but the wealthiest yachtsmen and are rarely seen beyond the racing circuit. They also have their limitations. Team Philips, the catamaran that was meant to carry Pete Goss around the world, was built using huge amounts of honeycomb sandwich, but unfortunately went on to break apart in the Atlantic during a storm.

NAUTICAL PUZZLES

If you are the skipper, then it it all comes down to you;
you mustn't ever lose me, or the crew will lose theirs too.
What am I?
Answer on page 145

SEEING THE LIGHT

Light signals at sea and how to tell them apart

Fixed (F) This light is constantly on and shines with steady intensity.

Flashing (Fl) The total duration of light is always less than the duration of the darkness.

Quick Flashing (Qk Fl) The light flashes between 50 and 79 times per minute. The total duration of light is shorter than darkness.

Very Quick Flashing (V Qk Fl) Between 80 and 159 flashes per minute, usually 100 or 120. The total duration of light is shorter than the darkness.

Interrupted Quick Flashing (I Qk Fl) Like Quick Flashing, but with one moment of darkness in one period.

Group Flashing (Gp Fl) A series of flashes followed by a period of darkness. A light which flashed three times would be shown as Gp Fl(3) on a British chart.

Long-Flashing (LFL) This light has one long flash in a period. A long flash is at least two seconds long.

Isophase (Iso) This light has equal duration between light and darkness. A period consists of both a light and a dark interval.

Occulting (Occ) Occulting is the opposite of flashing – the light is more on than off. Can be Group-occulting or Composite Group-occulting.

Alternating (Alt) An alternating light that changes colour. A light that flashes white and red would be marked Alt WR on a chart.

Morse (Mo) A light showing a letter from the Morse code alphabet, replacing dots and dashes with flashes and long flashes. The letter 'U' would be shown as a light flashing the Morse for 'U' (- - —), it would be recorded as Mo(U) on a chart and would show two flashes followed by a long flash.

23

Yachtsmen like to race. Some do so unofficially, tweaking their sails to try to catch up with the boat in front of them as they cruise down the coast. Others race only occasionally, taking part in an annual club event. But there are many sailors who take to the water only in order to compete.

If the racing is organised, and the fleet made up of different designs, then a handicapping system is needed to create a level playing field so the yachts can compete with some kind of parity.

Handicapping is the way in which race committees attempt to allow slow boats to race against fast boats and declare which boat was sailed the best. That at least is the theory. The reality involves huge amounts of confusion, rule-bending, arguments, calculations and occasional skullduggery.

There are almost as many handicapping systems as there are international racing committees. Each looks at the yachts that race in its events and adopts the system that works best. Yachts may be handicapped according to a complex set of calculations taking into consideration sail area, length, weight, hull shape and other factors to produce a rating. The International Measurement System is one such system that has been widely adopted.

The problems start as soon as the formula is declared. Designers and victory-hungry sailors start to tear it apart, looking for loopholes that they can exploit. A few years later, yachts start to emerge from boatyards with exaggerated shapes. The stern may be very narrow, a huge bowsprit may have been added, odd attachments may have blossomed on keels.

All these changes are designed to make the boat go faster without affecting the handicap. If the designers are successful, there are only two options for the race committee. They can either accept the changes and thus oblige all the other skippers to copy them if

24

they wish to remain competitive, or change the rules to outlaw the new designs. Whichever route they decide to take, there will be many unhappy yachtsmen.

Such wrangling is inevitable with any form of yacht handicapping system and sailors have got used to it. Those who wish to promote the sport have taken an alternative route. When all the yachts are the same there are no problems with handicapping. The first over the line is the winner. The public can understand what's going on and so are more likely to watch the action, and sponsors are therefore easier to attract. Sometimes the simplest solutions are the best.

ROPE SIZES

Next time you go down to the chandlery,
this is what you can order (in inches)

Diameter	Circumference
¼	¾
⅜	1¼
½	1½
⅝	2
¾	2¼
⅞	2¾
1	3

TYPES OF ANCHOR

Grapnel
Bruce
Delta
Fisherman
Danforth
Plough
CQR (secure – geddit?)

SEA SAYINGS

Son of a gun

Sir Francis Drake once allowed a comely lass called Maria to sail on board the *Golden Hind*. Maria fell pregnant but the father of the child could have been anyone from the Captain down. Drake did the dishonourable thing and marooned her, for although taking women on board was common practice it was officially frowned open. If children were born aboard, the delivery often took place between guns on the gun deck. If the child's father was unknown, they were entered in the ship's log as 'son of a gun'.

BLOW ME!

Sails can work in one of two ways. Imagine Tom Sawyer and Huckleberry Finn on their raft with a bed sheet rigged up as a sail and the wind exactly behind them, blowing them along. That simple pushing motion is how the most basic sails work and is also how yachts are driven straight downwind by their giant, colourful spinnakers.

When the wind is not behind them, modern sails work more like the wings of an aeroplane. They are made so that they become curved when the wind blows over them. Some even have huge batons that keep them permanently curved. This shape creates greater pressure on the windward side of the sail than on the leeward (downwind) side. This pressure difference keeps a plane in the sky and drives a yacht through the water, helped by the shape of the hull.

Yachts were built with wings instead of sails in the late 20th century, with mixed results, but designers have not given up and the fastest sailing vessels on the planet being built today have solid, vertical wings instead of traditional sails.

THE CURSE OF THE COCKROACH

Watch yachtsmen loading stores in their boats in sunny climes and you'll observe a strange ritual. Each item is taken out of the bag or box and carefully inspected. Only once it is certified 'cockroach free' is it stowed away.

Ridding a yacht of cockroaches is near impossible. Unlike houses, with their regular four-walled rooms, yachts are full of nooks and crannies where these beasties can hide away and breed. They come aboard hidden in food and packaging, or as eggs in cardboard boxes – many sailors ban cardboard for this very reason. Others soak bunches of bananas over the side for half an hour to ensure any visitors swim away or drown.

If the worst happens and cockroaches get past your defences, chemical warfare is one solution. Boric acid mixed with sugar should do the trick. A more extreme option is a fumigation bomb – open lockers and drawers, throw in the bomb, close the hatches and leave the boat for a day. A further treatment will be required two weeks later to kill off any newly-hatched roaches.

A more environmentally-friendly solution comes with eight legs. Certain spiders, such as the US Housekeeper, eat cockroaches for breakfast, lunch and dinner. Although nautical arachnophobes may not be happy, the spider reportedly keeps a low profile once on board.

HOW TO READ A BAROMETER

Every yacht should have a barometer on board. The rule of thumb is the higher the pressure the more settled the weather, and vice versa.

Falling steadily	A sign of bad weather
Rising steadily	A sign of good weather
Falling rapidly	Bad weather and gales coming soon
Rising rapidly	Better weather, but it may be short-lived

BUOYS WILL BE BUOYS

There are six different types of buoy at sea and each is used for different purposes. As well as the shape of the buoy itself, further information as to its use can be gathered from the colour of the buoy and the shapes of any marks that are attached to it.

 1 CONICAL – looks like a pointed cone; typically used for unlit buoys to starboard.

 2 CAN/CYLINDRICAL – looks like a cylinder on end; typically used for unlit buoys to port.

 3 SPHERICAL – the part above the water-line is shaped like a sphere; typically used as unlit safe water or mid-channel buoys.

 4 PILLAR – typically a lattice tower mounted on a flat base; used just about anywhere, commonly as a base on which to mount a light.

 5 SPAR – in the form of a pole, or a long cylinder, floating upright; used just about anywhere, commonly with a light.

 6 BARREL – looks like a cylinder on its side; used only as a special mark.

THE PERILS OF SEAFARING

'Excuse me,' called Douglas, 'you don't have any water, do you? It's just that our canoe seems to be on fire.'

I THINK I'LL BUILD MY BOAT WITH...

Ferro cement

Ferro cement arrived at around the same time as Glass Reinforced Plastic (GRP) but has not proved so successful. On paper it has a lot going for it: cheap, strong, durable, impervious to rot, rust, worms and osmosis – and it is easy to build with by yourself. It was this last 'advantage' that has crippled rather than created demand for Ferro cement boats. Many boats were built in back gardens across the length and breadth of the country. Some went on to sail the world, others never made it past the first stages of construction. Those that did were often incredibly heavy, due to liberal applications of Ferro cement. Boat-builders frequently created huge hulls because the material was so cheap, then discovered that they could not afford the proportionately more expensive fixtures and fittings. Very few boats are built of Ferro cement these days.

ALL DRESSED UP

Dressing overall is the yachting equivalent of putting on the glad rags and involves hoisting a string of flags from the bow, up to the top of the mast, then down to the stern. It is now common for all sorts flags to be flown in any order – but if you want to do it properly, then here's how:

E, Q, 3, G, 8, Z, 4, W, 6, P, 1, I, Code, T, Y,
B, X, 1st Sub, H, 3rd Sub, D, F, 2nd Sub, U, A,
O, M, R, 2, J, 0, N, 9, K, 7, V, 5, L, C, S.

SAILING TERMS THAT CONFUSE LANDLUBBERS

Angel

The word 'angel' may conjure up images of cherubim and seraphim floating on clouds, but an angel on a boat is likely to be muddy, rusty, underwater and possibly made of lead. At sea, an angel is a weight attached to an anchor chain to make it more effective. Suspended halfway along its length, an angel ensures the pull on the anchor is more horizontal than vertical. It also makes the motion of an anchored vessel more gentle and limits her swinging circle.

HOW POSH

Before the advent of discount airlines, if you wanted to journey to a far continent you had to do so by boat. It would take months to sail to India or Australia and cabins that faced the afternoon sun could become intolerably hot. The cooler, shaded side of the boat was on the port side as you headed south to the colonies, and on the starboard side as you headed back. Of course a premium had to be paid for such luxury and only the smartest could travel Port Out Starboard Home – or POSH as it became known.

Taking to the high seas for pleasure is a relatively recent trend – little more than 150 years old. Nakedness has been around for much longer, of course, but has largely fallen out of favour in modern times. But many of today's yachtsmen can often be found at the helm wearing nothing but a smile. Luckily there is so much sea out there that it is very easy to find a patch of it that is all your own and far from prying eyes. The curvature of the earth means that one has to venture only a few miles offshore before dipping beyond the horizon and into a private world where clothes are entirely optional.

For the long-distance yachtsman, nakedness is almost a necessity. Once clothes get wet with seawater they will never truly dry until rinsed in fresh water – a precious commodity. Having damp, salty clothes next to your skin spells trouble in the form of sores and boils. No clothes means no rubbing and no sores – problem solved.

Certain sailing vessels attract more nudity than others. Most famous are the Wharram catamarans, twin-hulled boats that come in a range of lengths and sizes (as do their owners). Designer James Wharram promotes a philosophy of cooperative construction and maximum nudity and can regularly be found in the pages of the yachting press extolling the virtues of nakedness on board.

Nudity at sea is not without its problems. First, you need good weather – no sailor enjoys fighting a sou'westerly gale in nothing but their birthday suit. Secondly, you need the right company – beware any yachts looking for crew if the skipper has a beard, a deep tan and a strange glint in his eye. Thirdly, you must take care of your behind. Sitting naked in a fibreglass boat encourages sweating and presents the risk of slipping overboard, while a wooden boat will breathe beneath your buttocks but splinters are a constant hazard.

THE NATIONAL MARITIME MUSEUM, GREENWICH

The National Maritime Museum (NMM) was formally established by Act of Parliament in 1934 and opened to the public by King George VI on 27 April 1937. It includes the 17th-century Queen's House and, since the 1950s, the Royal Observatory. There is also a small museum at Cotehele Quay on the Tamar, Cornwall, with the NMM/National Trust sailing barge *Shamrock*, and the Valhalla ships' figurehead collection on Tresco, Isles of Scilly.

The collections comprise about 2.48 million items, many on loan to museums elsewhere in Britain. The public galleries at Greenwich display a selection and the remainder are accessible for public interest and research in various ways. From December 2002 the majority of the NMM small-boat collection has been on display at the new National Maritime Museum, Cornwall, in Falmouth.

The museum has the most important collection in the world recording the history of Britain at sea, including maritime art, cartography, manuscripts and official public records, ship models and plans, scientific and navigational instruments, and timekeeping and astronomical instruments (based at the Observatory). Its collection of British portraits is exceeded in size only by the National Portrait Gallery, and its holdings related to Nelson and Cook, among many others, are unrivalled. The museum also boasts the world's largest maritime historical reference library (100,000 volumes), on the shelves of which you can find books dating back as far as the 15th century.

The museum buildings are also of great architectural importance: the Queen's House in particular is one of the keystones of the historic park-and-palace landscape of Maritime Greenwich, which was deemed a UNESCO World Heritage Site in 1997.

COASTAL CRUISING FIRST AID KIT

A few essentials for all eventualities

For common problems
Antacid tablets, Aspirin, Bandage, Peptic relief tablets, Provodine iodine, Thermometer (unbreakable)

Dressing pads, Gauze pads, Iodine, Razor (disposable), Roll gauze, Skin stapler (disposable), Skin staple remover, Synthetic gloves, Transparent wound covers

For minor trauma
Adhesive tape, Bandage, Fingertip bandage, Knuckle bandage, BZK antiseptic wipes, Gauze pads, Hydrogen peroxide, Paramedic shears, Triple antibiotic ointment, Tweezers with magnifier

Burns
Burn pads, Burn wraps, Sterile gauze

For major lacerations
Adhesive tape, Benzoin swabs, Butterfly enclosures,

For sprains and fractures
Adhesive tape, Splint (15in), Elastic bandage, Finger splint, Ice bags, Ice tape, Safety pins, Triangle sling

System problems
Alcohol prep pads, Calamine lotion, Cotton swabs, Elastic bandage, Eye wash and pads, Scalpel, Sting aid wand

CPR
CPR mask with valve, Oral airways device, Synthetic gloves

WHAT LIES BENEATH

The colour of the sea is largely dictated by the nature of the seabed and how deep the water is. This simple rhyme offers practical advice to the uncertain sailor:

> *Brown brown, run aground,*
> *White white, you might,*
> *Green green, nice and clean,*
> *Blue blue, run right through.*

MAYDAY!

The word 'mayday' derives from the French phrase for 'Help me' – 'M'aidez'. A mayday call is the most urgent distress call that a vessel can broadcast and is used where a boat or person is threatened by grave and imminent danger and requires immediate assistance.

This is the mayday procedure recommended by *Reed's Nautical Almanac*:

- Check main battery switch is on
- Switch radio on, and select high power (25 watts)
- Select VHF Ch 16 (or 2182 kHz for MF)
- Press and hold down the transmit button, and say slowly and distinctly:
- 'Mayday, mayday, mayday'
- 'This is…' (name of boat, spoken three times)
- 'Mayday…' (name of boat spoken once)
- 'My position is…' (latitude and longitude, or true bearing and distance from a known point)
- Nature of distress (sinking, on fire, etc)
- Aid required (immediate assistance)
- Number of persons on board
- Any other important, helpful information (eg, if yacht is drifting, whether distress flares are being fired)
- 'Over'

On completion of the distress message, release the transmit button and listen.

THE COASTAL NAVIGATOR'S BASIC KIT

Binoculars • Chart • Course-plotter
Dividers (drawing compasses) • Steering compass
Electronic log • GPS set • Handbearing compass
Pencils • Rubber • Ruler • Stopwatch

CAPTAIN PUGWASH IS INNOCENT

It's widely, but incorrectly, believed that Captain Pugwash, a cartoon originally broadcast on the BBC between 1958 and 1967, featured characters including Master Bates, Seaman Staines and Roger the Cabin Boy. In fact, the crew on the Black Pig were called Master Mate and Tom the Cabin Boy, and fellow pirates were named Barnabas and Willy. John Ryan, Captain Pugwash's creator, won retractions and settlements from the *Sunday Correspondent* and *The Guardian* after both newspapers claimed that the show's characters had names worth sniggering over.

QUAY MOMENTS IN NAUTICAL HISTORY

It was when construction was finished that they realised why the docks in Rugby were so much cheaper than those by the sea.

THE ALLURE OF BOATING

Sandra's 'Introduction to Oarsmanship' classes had proved popular with even the club's most experienced members.

CRUISING COCKTAILS

Smooth Sailing

This long refreshing cocktail is popular with yachtsmen on the other side of the Pond. It slips down easily – very easily – so be careful that it is only the drink that ends up on the rocks.

To mix, take a good shot of vodka and add an equal amount of Triple Sec. Pour both over ice and top up with equal parts of orange juice and cranberry juice. If you own a motor boat or a humourously named yacht, you may wish to drizzle cherry brandy over the top.

SWALLOWS AND AMAZONS FOREVER!

Arthur Ransome's *Swallows and Amazons* books, first published in the 1930s, introduced many young children to sailing. The main characters were two groups of children who go sailing, camping and exploring in the Lake District.

Swallows: John • Susan • Titty • Roger • Bridget
Amazons: Nancy • Peggy

MAN OVERBOARD

Falling overboard from a yacht is a life-threatening situation, but there are some simple precautions that can maximise the chances of a safe recovery. It is now widely believed that furling the headsail and approaching the casualty under motor is the safest way to come alongside a MOB, but that is often just the start of the trouble. Lifelines at the stern of the boat should be secured with rope lashing, allowing them to be cut so that there is a clear space over which to haul the casualty. Recovery via a boarding ladder makes sense in calm conditions if the MOB is strong enough. If not, a dinghy or life raft can be used as a staging point before recovery. There are various man overboard slings on the market, but some of these have been shown to be dangerously inadequate. If you have one, make sure you've tried it out – there'll be no time to read the instructions with a man in the water.

One technique that has been known to work is to drop the boom into the cockpit and lower the mainsail out of its track on the mast and allow it to fall overboard, creating a giant sling in the water. If the casualty can clamber into this sling the halyard can then be winched up and the person raised and rolled on board. That's the theory – but again this technique should be practised in case you need it to save a life.

Modern round-the-world racing started with the Golden Globe race in 1968. The course ran south from Falmouth, around the Cape of Good Hope at the tip of Africa, continued beneath Australia, across the Southern Ocean, round Cape Horn, up the Atlantic and back to Blighty. The winner, Robin Knox-Johnston, was the only man to complete the course and became the first person to circumnavigate the world single-handed and without stopping. The journey took him 313 days.

Of the eight other competitors in the race, six failed to get beyond the Southern Atlantic. Chay Blyth was one of these competitors but later made up for his disappointment by sailing non-stop around the world in the opposite direction – against prevailing winds and currents. Probably the strangest tale is that of Donald Crowhurst, a troubled man who had set out to sea in spite of many misgivings and feelings of self-doubt. Instead of sailing round the world, Crowhurst hid off the coast of South America until his fellow competitors were on the final leg of the race, at which point he re-emerged and joined the others, claiming to have rounded both Capes. The skipper of the vessel just ahead of Crowhurst pushed his storm-battered yacht so hard that she broke up and he had to be rescued. Crowhurst, now likely to win the prize for the fastest passage, realsied that his deceit was certain to be discovered and, after leaving a rambling confession, he stepped overboard to his death.

The final entrant, Bernard Moitessier, did manage to sail round the world but decided against returning to Europe and just kept going, passing south of Australia for a second time before finally putting in at Tahiti after 37,455 miles and 301 days at sea.

MEDITERRANEAN WINDS AND WHERE THEY BLOW FROM

Northerly	*Tramontana*
North-easterly	*Greco*
Easterly	*Levante*
South-easterly	*Sirocco*
Southerly	*Ostro*
South-westerly	*Libeccio*
Westerly	*Ponente*
North-westerly	*Maestro*

THE BOTTOM CLEANERS

Spare the occasional thought for the bottom of your boat. All manner of animal and vegetable life makes its home on yachts' hulls – and the more that's there, the slower the boat will go. Antifouling paint will help slow down the growth but won't stop it altogether, which means a jolly good scrub is required from time to time. If you've got the money, ask the boatyard to crane the boat out and blast her with a high pressure hose. If you're strapped for cash you can go round in a dinghy with a deck brush – though you'll probably need to don swimming trunks and a mask to clean the keel.

There is an alternative, however, in the shape of the BoatScrubber. This cunning invention works like a car-wash for boats. You sail up to a pontoon, moor your yacht and hand over your money. Two large round brushes rise out from the water, detect where the vessel starts, and begin to spin. They work their way down each side of the hull, slowly but surely, and rid it of all the marine life that has been growing there. They can handle almost any sort of keel, but can't do the inner sides of catamarans. Once their work is complete they sink beneath the waves and you sail away with a lovely clean bottom.

SEEING RED

During New Zealand's successful America's Cup challenge in 1995, Kiwi skipper Peter Blake, who was later knighted, wore the same pair of red socks throughout as Team New Zealand went through the campaign winning all but one of their races. The only race they lost was when Blake was rested. Before the final, team sponsors manufactured tens of thousands of pairs of Blake's lucky red socks which sold out in days in New Zealand. They won the final, beating Dennis Connor's American team in a 5-0 drubbing. Blake was killed by pirates during an exploration of the Amazon River in 2001, but red socks are still associated with sailing and success in his homeland.

SAILING TERMS THAT CONFUSE LANDLUBBERS

Boom

Not what a cannon does, nor half of Basil Brush's laugh, the boom is the pole that extends horizontally from the bottom of the mast. The boom is positioned on most yachts at such a height that it will take the top of your head off in the same manner as one may remove the top of an egg. The most effective way to carry out such a marine lobotomy is by gybing, allowing the back of the boat to pass through the wind. This causes the boom, which holds the outside corner (or clew) of the mainsail, to swing through about 180 degrees in a split second, accelerating all the time. Gybes can be carried out in a controlled manner with the helmsman calling out a warning, then calling out 'Gybe-o' just before the boom swings across. Accidental gybes are more commonly accompanied by a curse, with the helmsman calling out 'Gybe-o' just after the boom has whistled millimetres past your ear.

WHAT A PRO

Procedural words, or 'prowords', are used in radio communications to increase the brevity and clarity of communications. As you will see, people only say 'Over and out' in the movies.

Say again	To ask for a repetition
I say again	To give a repetition
Correction	Said before correcting part of a message
Spell	Said before using the phonetic alphabet to spell a word
This is	To identify caller
Over	Invitation to reply
Out	The end of the conversation. No reply is expected.

GALE WARNINGS

In nautical parlance, a gale is a period of severe weather with winds of at least Force Eight (34–40 knots). If such winds (and the gusts reaching 43–51 knots that accompany them) are expected within a weather forecasting sea area, then a gale warning for that area will be issued. Severe gales involve winds of at least Force Nine (41–47 knots) and gusts of up to 60 knots. A storm occurs if winds reach Force 10 (48–55 knots) with gusts of up to 68 knots.

Gales that are described as 'imminent' are expected to arrive within six hours of the warning's time of issue. 'Soon' indicates an arrival within 6–12 hours and 'later' means more than 12 hours from time of issue.

Strong wind warnings are issued when winds of Force Six (22–27 knots) or above are expected up to five miles offshore.

Britain may not be a very big country but her coastline is extremely varied and there is a part of it that will suit every sailor. One can, very crudely, break up the principal sailing areas of the British Isles into broad regions. Here are the arguments for and against them.

West Country

Stretching from The Isles of Scilly, standing sentinel in the Atlantic, to the River Exe in Devon, there is no cruising ground like it in the British Isles – at least that it what the locals will tell you, though many yachtsmen from elsewhere also rate it as their favourite sailing spot. The coast is varied with sandy beaches, tall cliffs and plenty of wooded valleys up which rivers meander, creating perfect anchorages and sheltered harbours. Helford, Falmouth, Fowey, Plymouth, Salcombe, Dartmouth and Exmouth are all delightful and don't have the crowds synonymous with the waters around the Solent.

The South

More yachts are kept between Weymouth and Dover than in the rest of the country put together, and the majority of them are squeezed into marinas and on to moorings around the Solent. Fans of these waters will tell you of the convenience of it all, the variety of nearby harbours to visit, and the fact that there's always something going on. Detractors will point out the astronomical prices of marina berths, the crowded waters and the fact that you have to share the sea with huge shipping.

The East Coast

The southeastern corner of Britain is characterised in the minds of many sailors as flat and muddy, and parts of it do live up to this rather drab reputation. However, many of those who sail there would not swap it for anywhere else in the world. The network of rivers and estuaries, sandbanks and mudflats means that one can sail on the East Coast for a lifetime and never be bored. Having a boat that can settle on the mud is essential for fully exploring this potterer's paradise.

Western Scotland

Few yachtsmen make it this far but those who do declare it to be God's own cruising ground. The scenery is majestic with a backdrop of mountains and moorland that sweeps down to the sea. Compared with most other parts of the country you have the sea to yourself and can explore the numerous islands with their sandy beaches and snug anchorages protected from the swell of the open ocean. On the other hand it can be cold and it does rain an awful lot.

THE ALLURE OF LIFE AT SEA

Prince Albert liked his new pipe enormously, though smoking it always made his eyes water.

THE REALITY OF SAILING
The heads

The heads is what sailors call a lavatory on board a boat and there is nowhere else that the harsh, unromantic realities of sailing are more apparent.

Imagine the scene: you're at sea and the boat is heeled over. You've been on deck in your full oilskins and boots and now need to visit the heads. Your trousers have built-in braces meaning that you'll need to take your jacket off to get them down. This done, you are faced with a choice. Take off your oilskin trousers in the saloon (this will involve removing your boots too and getting your socks wet), or try to merely lower them to your ankles in the heads. You opt for the latter but find the toilet cubicle is so small, with so little elbow room, that the dexterity of a contortionist is required to achieve your goal.

Your trousers eventually dropped, you lower yourself towards the bowl, which rises and falls with the pitching boat. The toilet will have been set as low as possible so that your knees will be near your ears when you finally make contact. Now you have to remember to twist numerous stopcocks and flick various switches. Failure to do so will result in water flooding into the bowl and the boat sinking, or worse, the toilet blocking.

As you try and remember what to pump and when, the boat lurches and a wave of whatever is in the bowl splashes up against you. You hastily complete your business and man the pump to flush the bowl. But woe of woes! There is a blockage somewhere in the yards of too-thin pipe that snake from the loo to the sea. With a heavy heart you recall the ominous warning during the skipper's briefing: 'You block it, you clear it.'

HOW CHILLING

Low temperatures combined with strong winds can create a dangerous cocktail for those at sea. There are officially seven levels of wind chill factor:

I   Comfortable with normal precautions.
II   Work becomes uncomfortable on overcast days unless properly clothed.
III   Work becomes hazardous. Heavy clothing is necessary.
IV   Unprotected skin will freeze with direct exposure over a long period.
V   Unprotected skin will freeze within one minute.
VI   Adequate face protection is mandatory. Work alone is prohibited.
VII   Survival efforts are required.

THE PERILS OF THE SEA

'Yes Miss Jones. it was a very good dive,
but please don't do that again.'

NAUTICAL PUZZLES

1 Pick a number between 1 and 10 (including 1 or 10).
2 Multiply your number by 9.
3 Add together the two digits that make up the number created in step two.
4 Subtract 5 from the number created in step three.
5 Find the letter in the alphabet that corresponds to the number created in step four, ie: 1=A, 2=B, 3=C, etc.
6 Pick a country in Europe that starts with the letter you found in step five.
7 Pick a part of a yacht that starts with the last letter of your country.
8 Pick a colour that starts with the last letter of your yacht part.

Turn to page 145 to find out what sort of boat you sail.

MAKING WAVES

Why, in reality, sail always gives way to power.

If you spend enough time afloat you will learn all these things the hard way.

Always put on your oilskin jacket as soon as you think of it The same is said about reefing a sail, but the jacket is much more important. Yachtsmen often ignore this piece of advice and consequently only don a jacket after a stray wave has sploshed against the hull and down their neck.

Work out where the wind is coming from There are many ways to do this. The wind and waves generally come from the same direction, as do clouds. There's likely to be a wind indicator atop the mast and even a display on the instrument panel in the cockpit. You can even lick a finger, hold it up and see which direction feels cooler. If in doubt, ask. This is important because only when you know where the wind is coming from can you throw the dregs of your tea (or have a pee) in the opposite direction with confidence.

Obey the rules about the heads A ship's toilet can be temperamental and if the skipper tells you to rotate three times and say a prayer before you use it, then do so. Likewise, the rule about pumping 30 times when flushing means exactly that. You might think that everyone is going over the top with the whole flushing thing, but that may be because you have never spent a long time on a boat with a smelly loo or had to clear a bad blockage.

Stow everything Those on land talk of storage, those on boats speak of stowage. The concepts are identical except for one important factor: stowage is storage at 30 degrees of heel. Whenever you put something down you have to imagine the boat bashing to windward, heeled over on her side. Such violent movements turn shelves into ski jumps and cupboards into catapults. In such conditions only stowage in a seaworthy fashion will suffice.

THE ONLY WAY IS UP

The compass is perhaps the yachtsman's greatest friend, but all is not lost if your trusty compass goes over the side – as long as you're wearing a watch you'll be all right and will be able to tell which hemisphere you're in.

Hold the watch flat and point the hour hand at the sun. The line bisecting the angle made between the hour hand and the figure 12 will point approximately south. The reciprocal of this line will be north. In the Southern Hemisphere the bisecting angle points north. If you got rid of your old watch in favour of a flashy digital model you will have to wait until nightfall to work out where you are going. In the Northern Hemisphere the full moon is South at midnight (GMT).

THE SYDNEY-HOBART RACE

The race from Sydney to Hobart in Tasmania is as important a fixture in the Australian racing calendar as the Fastnet Race is to British yachtsmen. The 630-mile event was first held in 1945 and soon became a classic with an international field. It takes place on Boxing Day and attracts some of the best yachtsmen in the world. And just as the Fastnet will always be associated with the event of 1979 when 15 lives were lost, so will the Sydney-Hobart be forever associated with the events of 1998.

The fleet of 115 boats was hit by a severe storm as it crossed the Bass Strait between the Australian mainland and Tasmania. An area of massive high pressure, known as a 'bomb', had formed and winds of 78mph were reported, kicking up seas as high as 10m (33ft).

A total of 55 yachtsmen had to be rescued. Seven yachts were abandoned, five of which subsequently sank. Only 44 boats reached the finish line and six yachtsmen never made it back to dry land.

WHEN IS A KNOT NOT A KNOT?

When it has another name:

Angler's loop
Clinging clara
Duncan loop
Englishman's loop
Eskimo bowline
Fisherman's bend
Granny knot
Highwayman's hitch
Italian hitch
Surgeon's knot
Turk's head
Waggoner's hitch

ROYALTY AT A PRICE

If you fancy going for a sail but want to do so in style and not sacrifice your creature comforts, then why not sign up for a cruise on the $40 million *Royal Clipper*? She's a five-masted sailing ship – the only one in the world – and unlike on some cruising vessels, the sails actually work. The five tonnes of canvas that she can hoist cover an area of nine tennis courts and drive her through the water at 17 knots. Most of the 42 sails can be hoisted or furled via computer-controlled hydraulic winches, meaning that crew rarely need to climb the rigging. Beneath the sails are 228 cabins boasting all the luxuries of life that one could ask for. Restaurants offer the finest cuisine served in opulent surroundings, giving the passengers the best of both worlds – the romance of sail with the comfort of a cruise liner. And the price for all this luxury? £12,000 per person per week – the price of a secondhand yacht.

WHAT COLOUR ARE YOUR WELLIES?

There are some rules about what colour wellies should be worn where, and all sailors would do well to observe them. People who work in the country wear black wellies. Those who live there – or would like to – wear green wellies. Blue wellies are reserved for use at sea and in no circumstances should be worn more than a mile inland. Red wellies are worn only by children jumping in puddles and Frenchmen. Yellow wellies have been worn at sea, but not in the last 30 years. Despite the fact that a good quality rubber boot was adequate for generations of sailors, the modern yottie is shunning rubber in favour of various breathable materials. Mixtures of GoreTex (blue) and leather (brown) are popular, but expect to pay £200 or more to keep your feet dry.

CATAMARAN

The word 'catamaran' comes from two Tamil words: 'katta', meaning to bind or tie, and 'maram', meaning wood. The word is now commonly used for a two-hulled vessel, whether it be a cross-channel ferry, a beach cat like the popular Hobie 16, or a world-girdling, record-breaking, racing machine like Steve Fossett's *Playstation*.

The very first catamarans are thought to have been rafts of three or more logs tied together by natives of Sri Lanka. Strangely, the word was also used to refer to a British invention that was briefly popular at the start of the nineteenth century: a lead-lined box that contained explosives and a timing mechanism to create a sort of mine, which was used against the French with limited success. The term 'catamaran' was also given to small rectangular craft that acted as a buffer between a large vessel and a harbour wall. None of these cats should be confused with Cat Boats, which are single-hulled craft used for fishing in the shallow waters around Cape Cod.

THE MARY ROSE

The *Mary Rose* is the only sixteenth century warship on display anywhere in the world. Built between 1509 and 1511, she was one of the first ships able to fire a broadside, and was a firm favourite of King Henry VIII. The *Mary Rose* had a keel length of 32m and a breadth of 11.66m. Her length at the waterline is estimated to have been 38.5m and her draught 4.6m. After a long and successful career, she sank accidentally during an engagement with the French fleet in 1545. Her rediscovery and raising were seminal events in the history of nautical archaeology.

The search for and discovery of the *Mary Rose* was a result of the dedication of one man, the late Alexander McKee. In 1965, in conjunction with the South-sea branch of the British Sub-Aqua Club, he initiated project Solent Ships. While on paper this was a plan to examine a number of known wrecks in the Solent, Alex McKee really hoped to find the *Mary Rose*. He succeeded in 1967, and the *Mary Rose* was placed on a special cradle and lifted from the seabed in 1982. After painstaking restoration work she was put on display in Portsmouth.

CRUISING COCKTAILS

Salty Dog

A simple cocktail using ingredients that one may actually have on board. Take a glass and moisten the rim, then invert onto a saucer of salt. Add one measure of gin and top up with grapefruit juice. If time is short, dispense with the salt as most things on board are already encrusted in it.

Vodka can be used as a substitute for gin, as can rum, whisky and most fuel additives. If required, replace grapefruit juice with orange juice, apple juice, water or more gin.

THE MYSTERY OF THE MARY CELESTE

There are many myths and strange tales associated with the sea, but the one that has best stood the test of the time is the mystery of the *Mary Celeste*.

Built in 1860, *Mary Celeste* was a 103ft-long ocean-going sailing vessel. On 7 November 1872, she set off from New York. On board was Captain Briggs, his wife and young daughter, and a crew of eight. The hold was filled with 1,700 barrels of raw American alcohol, bound for Genoa.

On 4 December she was sighted by another vessel. As it drew near, it became apparent that the *Mary Celeste* was deserted. Her logbook ended 10 days earlier and her recorded position was more than 400 miles from where she was found. Could this ghost ship have sailed so far by herself? It seemed impossible. Her sails were properly set on the starboard side, but according to her logbook, the sails should have been set to port. The changing direction of the wind

meant that someone must have been onboard to tack her and reset the sails, and within the last few days. But who? Or what?

And what of the captain, his family and the crew? Accounts vary – some say that there was no evidence of foul play, others describe blood-smattered sails and cutlasses lying on deck. Some say that the ship's rowing boat was missing – could the crew have murdered Briggs and escaped? It would surely have been suicide to cast off in a small boat in the mid-Atlantic.

Could a giant wave have swept everyone overboard? Unlikely. Had they been attacked by pirates? But then why was the valuable cargo untouched. So many questions, so few answers.

The story of the *Mary Celeste* has proved a fascination for over 100 years. Sea monsters, sea quakes, alien abduction – they all have their adherents and the more the *Mary Celeste* is investigated, the more mysterious the story becomes.

SOME FACTS ABOUT SALT

The sea is made up of about 96.5% water and 3.5% dissolved salts. Salinity was once measured in parts per thousand but modern techniques now rely on electrical conductivity which gives rise to a number that indicates how salty a substance is.

The average salinity of the open ocean is around 35, although this can drop to as low as five where it is diluted by rivers, melting ice or very high rainfall. By contrast the water of the Red Sea can be as high as 40. The oceans are generally less salty around the poles, although there is also a band of low salinity around the equator. The North Atlantic is the saltiest large body of open ocean.

NAUTICAL PUZZLES

Which of the following is not a type of
double-ended dugout?
Kaep • Popo • Pungy
Tsukpin • Wa Lap
Answer on page 145

BENEATH THE WAVES

With their lack of gills and fins, men have generally pre-ferred travelling on top of the water rather than beneath it. However, there are records to suggest that simple sub-marines were thought of as early as 1578. It is unlikely that such vessels were ever constructed, but less than 50 years later a Dutchman named Cornelius Drebbel is believed to have built a watertight vessel with the minimum of positive buoyancy. The boat was driven by 12 oars which emerged through sealed holes and the oarsmen could drive the craft beneath the waves by changing the angle of the oars' blades.

BUOY, OH BUOY!

It would seem common sense for navigation buoys to follow a standardised system so that wherever you sail you'd know whether, for example, you should pass to starboard or to port of a green buoy as you enter a harbour.

The marine rule makers tried to come up with such a system but failed. Their compromise was to agree a system in which the same buoys mean totally contradictory things depending on where in the world you are.

In the 1970s the International Association of Lighthouse Authorities (IALA) came up with an agreement about five types of buoy – lateral, cardinal, isolated danger, safe water and special – with specific rules for each. Of the five types, the most common are those using the lateral system. The madness came when lighthouse authorities were allowed the choice of using red to mean 'go to the left of me' or 'go the right of me' on a regional basis. It's like a red traffic light meaning 'go' in one part of the world and 'stop' in another.

So it is that in Europe, Asia, Africa and Australasia a green buoy tells the sailor to do one thing and in the Americas and the Caribbean it tells them to do the opposite.

SEEING RED

Red sun at night, sailors delight;
Red sky in the morning, sailors take warning.

On a normal day the sun appears red as it sets and is orange when it pops up the next morning. Changes to these colours tell sailors (and shepherds too) that some sort of weather disturbance is on its way. If the morning sun seems very red, the air it is shining through will be unusually dry, cold air, and it is safe to predict that wind and rain will soon follow.

THE BEAUTY OF S&S

Sparkman and Stephens are synonymous with excellence in yacht design. S&S, as the partnership is better known, came about when the Stephens brothers, Olin and Rod, joined forces with Drake Sparkman in the late 1920s. The dominance of their designs has been unparalleled, from 6-, 8- and 12-metre boats to America's Cup yachts. Cruising yachts from the drawing board of Sparkman and Stephens are almost guaranteed to be fast, stable, safe and strong.

The team produced many racing yachts which are acknowledged classics – a number of which are still being raced. Photographs of beautiful S&S yachts such as *Dorade, Vim, Nyala, Columbia, Stormy Weather, Intrepid* and *Courageous* fill many a stunning coffee table book, yet pride and trust in your vessel are not restricted to these craft – they come as standard with any Sparkman and Stephens design.

CROSSING THE LINE

Crossing the equator is an unforgettable moment for any yachtsman. Not only does it mark their passing from one hemisphere to another, it also is likely to involve their being smeared with all manner of foul-smelling nasties before receiving a bucket of water over the head.

Such humiliating rituals stretch back into the mists of nautical history but are still keenly followed today, especially if there is someone on board who still remembers their own initiation. The style of ceremony varies from vessel to vessel but should involve someone dressed up as King Neptune who presides over proceedings and before whom the equator virgins are paraded. Neptune gives his orders, the gunk is administered and everyone has a drink and a laugh. If only all royal courts were such fun.

GO TO SEA ON A 'C'

A surprising number of types of boat begin with a letter 'C'

Cableship   vessel fitted for laying underwater cable
Caique   small traditional Turkish or Greek sailing boat
Camship   merchant ship armed with catapult to launch a plane
Canoa   sloop-rigged fishing boat from Brazil
Canoe   narrow open boat, powered by paddles or sails
Capital ship   the most important warship in a navy's fleet
Caracore   fast Indonesian sailing vessel
Caravel   small Mediterranean trading vessel
Cargo ship   vessel carrying freight rather than passengers
Carrack   large European trading vessel with high fore and aft castles
Cartel   ship used in times of war to negotiate between enemies
Casco   small, flat-bottomed cargo boat from the Philippines
Catamaran   any twin-hulled vessel
Cat boat   beamy, shallow sailing boat from Cape Cod in the USA
Chasse-Marée   lugger used by French customs and pirates
Clipper   very fast sailing ships of the 19th century
Coaster   any vessel employed in coastal trade
Coble   flat-bottomed fishing boat from north-east England
Cock boat   any boat carried on board another
Cog   merchant ship of the 15th century
Coracle   small boat made from stretching skins over a wicker frame
Corbita   merchant ship of Imperial Rome
Corvette   flush-decked warship of the 18th century
Cromster   two-masted Elizabethan vessel
Cunner   dug-out canoe with two sails
Cutter   yacht with a mainsail and two foresails

SAILING TERMS THAT CONFUSE LANDLUBBERS

Log

Another of those words that means several things at sea, including a large chunk of wood, as in 'Oh dear we've just hit a log.' Precisely speaking, a ship's log is the device that records the distance a vessel has travelled. Such distances are recorded in a log-book, commonly shortened to log. This is the sort of log made famous by the captain of the Starship Enterprise. The ship's log contains all the details of where you have been, where you are now and where you are going. As well as positions, courses and speeds, the responsible skipper will note down the weather forecast and any other relevant information. Some log-books are works of science, some are works of fiction that have been filled in after arrival for the sake of appearances, while others are works of art, complete with sketches of the local flora and fauna. The use of the word originates from the floating, wooden sort of log that was thrown overboard with a knotted line attached and used to calculate a vessel's speed.

LITTLE BOATS THAT CROSSED THE ATLANTIC

Year	Boat name	Length	Skipper	Time
1964	Sjo Ag	12ft	John Riding	67 days
1966	Nonoalca	12ft	Bill Verity	66 days
1968	April Fool	5ft 11¾in	Hugo Vilhen	84 days
1979	Yankee Girl	10ft	Gerry Spiess	54 days
1981	Soddim*	9ft	Christian Marty	37 days
1982	Giltspur	9ft 9in	Tom McClean	50 days
1982	Windswill	9ft	Bill Dunlop	76 days
1982	Toniky-Nou	5ft 10in	Eric Peters	46 days

a windsurfer

SLOW DOWN!

Speed is generally regarded as a good thing for any yachtsman. Whether racing around the buoys or cruising from port to port, most sailors have their boats sailing as quickly as possible. There are, however, rare instances when too much speed can be a bad thing.

If a yachtsman is caught out by rough weather and finds himself at sea with huge waves and high winds, then thoughts turn to survival. Sailing into the wind is likely to result in damage to the boat; running before the wind – in the same direction as the winds and waves – reduces the pressures on yacht and crew but carries its own dangers. Yachts are lifted by the waves and surf down them, gathering speed. The faster the boat goes, the greater the risk that she will be pushed sideways with a wave powering down on her and possibly rolling her over.

Reducing the vessel's speed is the key to survival. In such extreme circumstances sails will have been lowered, the wind blowing on the yacht's mast and hull being enough to drive her through the water.

A variety of objects can be towed to act as a brake. These are known as drogues and include very long lengths of rope, each end secured to the stern with the loop being dragged behind, small sails or even a car tyre or two. Purpose-made drogues look like parachutes made of canvas straps.

NAUTICAL PUZZLES

You are sailing down the Atlantic from Britain to South America. You do not have any means of electronic navigation, and the sky is constantly obscured by clouds so that the sun, moon and stars are never visible. How do you know when you have crossed the equator?
Answer on page 145

SEA SAYINGS

First rate

From the 16th century until steam-powered ships took over, British naval ships were rated as to the number of heavy cannon they carried. A ship of 100 or more guns was a First Rate line-of-battle ship. Second Rates carried 90 to 98 guns; Third Rates 64 to 89 guns; Fourth Rates 50 to 60 guns. Frigates carrying 20 to 48 guns were Fifth- and Sixth-rated.

THREE SHEETS TO THE WIND

Classic pub names with a nautical theme

The Albion • The Bell • The Blue Anchor
Bramley Moore • The Britannia • The British Pilot
The Chase • Diver's Arms • Hope Inn • The Kelly
Look Out • Lord Nelson • Man o'War • The Marine
The Monarch • Neptune Inn • The New Ferry Tavern
Old Endeavour • Royal Oak • The Ship
The Stack • The Telegraph • The Trafalgar

RECOMMENDED ANCHOR WEIGHTS

Anchor type	Yacht length (feet)	Recommended weight (kilos)
Bruce	32	5
	46	10
CQR	30–40	9–11
	40–50	11–16
Delta	30–40	10
	40–50	16
Danforth	36	7.3
	45	19
Spade	34	15
	51	20

If disaster befalls you in home waters, the odds are that you won't have to wait too long before being rescued. Things are different if you're in the middle of the ocean. In such a scenario, water must be your first concern. If you have enough water you will probably live. Without it you will certainly die. If you are stuck at sea for long enough your reserves of water will eventually run out. Many ocean-going yachtsmen now carry water makers on board that can extract drinking water from the sea. However they can be very inefficient and are not always reliable – but don't despair. Look to the heavens instead because that's where salvation lies in the form of rainwater. If you wait long enough the skies will open and you'll need to be ready to make the most of it. Various techniques can be employed to catch rainwater and you don't need disaster to strike before you try them out. Water that hits sails can be channelled to run off one area and simple canvas rain-catchers can be made to trap this water and lead it to a storage container. Special catchers can also be stretched out between the winches in the cockpit and the collected water led via a pipe to the cabin – allowing water to be caught without the crew getting drenched.

The simplest method of all is to allow the first few moments of rain to wash the decks of salt and debris and then to remove the cap to the yacht's water tank. This is usually positioned on the edge of the side deck, meaning that water running aft will flow straight into the tank. It may be necessary to direct the flow to make sure as much water as possible ends up in the tank.

By using techniques such as these many sailors have survived certain death through dehydration while others have been able to voyage to lands that would otherwise have been beyond their reach.

SAILING TERMS THAT
CONFUSE LANDLUBBERS

Sheet

Crisp white sheets are never found on board boats, though salty and slightly damp ones may be. Real sailors eschew such fanciness and lie on the floor (or sole) in their oilskins in a sleeping bag. There is an altogether more important sort of sheet to be found on board a sailing boat – and it's not a sheet at all. It's a rope. To be more exact, it is the rope that pulls in – or lets out – a sail and will be tweaked almost constantly by the perfectionist yachtsman. To 'sheet in' is to pull in the sheet, and it is common practice to use the name of the sail to which the rope is tied as a prefix. Pulling in the mainsheet thus draws the mainsail towards the centre of the boat. Beware of shouting 'Sheet!' too loudly in French ports.

LAT OR LONG?

Distance at sea is another of those things that is more complicated than it first appears. A mile is a mile on land, but at sea it is defined as the length of one minute of latitude. As a result the length of a nautical mile varies from 6,108 feet at the Poles to 6,048 feet at the Equator. A standardised International nautical mile is 6,076 feet, or 1,852 metres.

While latitude changes slightly between the Equator and the Poles, longitude changes much more. One minute of longitude is roughly equal to one minute of latitude at the Equator, and at the Poles it is zero. If you think of the lines of longitude meeting at the top and bottom of a globe, you will soon understand why this is so. The longitude scale on a chart must therefore never be used to measure distance.

TRADITIONAL NAUTICAL MEASUREMENTS

1 fathom = six feet or two yards
1 cable = 608 feet, 200 yards or 100 fathoms
1 sea or nautical mile = 6,080 feet or 10 cables or
2,000 yards
1 knot = one sea mile per hour
1 knot = 1.15 land miles per hour

HOW TO GET KNOTTED

The clove hitch

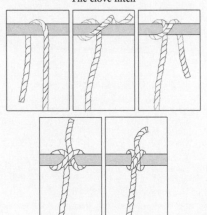

Pass a length of rope around the object (such as a spar) and then over again, crossing the working end of the rope over its standing part. Keeping the rope parallel to the first turn, tuck the working end underneath the second turn. Pull on both ends to tighten.

A HAPPY SHIP...

Given the choice of going to sea with an expert sailor or a good skipper, most people would pick the good skipper every time. The expert may be able to get the boat sailing faster, or plot its position to the nearest inch and tie a bowline with his teeth, but if he's not a good skipper too, it'll all be for nought.

Technical expertise can be learnt, but the people skills required of a good skipper are more important. Boats can be stressful places with wind howling through the rigging, waves breaking onto the deck, and the whole thing shifting up and down. A good skipper realises that calm is required, not additional stress. His commands are authoritative but polite. He instills confidence instead of making his crew wonder what all the fuss is about. Above all, the super skipper does not assume knowledge. 'Pull the red rope! The red one!' screams the expert sailor at his novice crew. 'I can't see a red one!' wails the crew. Our expert has forgotten that the 'red rope' is actually white with a red thread running through it.

Things happen slowly on a good skipper's boat. There's plenty of warning before anything is done and everyone is told what will happen and what he or she must do. The expert will be barking instructions as the boom swings across and the sails start to flap. The good skipper pours oil on troubled waters, the expert pours water on boiling oil.

But above and beyond all these niceties is the fact that the good skipper ensures that the kettle is always on and the tea keeps coming. That's the real secret to a happy ship.

NAUTICAL PUZZLES

Rearrange this household item to make a nautical calamity:
Verandah broom
Answer on page 145

IVAN THE TERRIBLE

The Caribbean is a yachtsman's paradise. Warm seas, beautiful beaches, fresh winds, stunning anchorages, colourful local culture – it's got it all. However, it does have one drawback – it lies within the hurricane belt. Each year these meteorological menaces sweep northwards, leaving a trail of destruction. The path of each hurricane is carefully recorded and some of the Caribbean islands are considered beyond their reach – or at least they were.

Grenada was one such island, and hundreds of yachts would dock in its southern boat-yards each year at the insistence of insurers to spend the hurricane season below the 12 degree line of latitude that passes through the island. Not any more. In the autumn of 2004, Hurricane Ivan swept Grenada reaping chaos. Yachts were toppled like dominoes – hardly any were left standing as 150mph winds battered the island. Millions of pounds' worth of damage was caused to yachts that were often the only home of cruising couples who had 'sold up and sailed away' to follow their dream.

The impact on the island's population was terrible, with thirty-nine people killed, 90% of homes destroyed and looters running riot in the streets. As the winds finally subsided, scores of boat-owners emerged to find their vessels destroyed. Tales emerged of crews swimming ashore with ropes to secure their boats and being trapped in mangrove swamps as the air became thick with flying debris. One skipper stayed on board and could not believe his luck as his yacht was dragged out to sea and then blown safely back to shore after the eye of the storm passed.

The sailors' lack of preparation for the hurricane was understandable. It had been some 49 years since a storm of such strength had hit Grenada. Now no one will say when the next one will come.

MARITIME MARRIAGES

*Charles tried to block his ears to Sarah's complaints.
Rowing across the Atlantic was certainly not the
dream honeymoon he had imagined.*

OIL ON TROUBLED WATERS

The thought of filling a canvas bag with fish oil on the deck
of a storm-tossed ship may be one that does not appeal, yet
this stinking bag may be the key to your survival. Breaking
seas pose the greatest risk to a boat in a storm and a layer
of oil over the surface of the water helps prevent these dangerous waves – hence the phrase 'pour oil on troubled
waters'. Here's how you do it: take a heavy canvas bag
about 30cm by 60cm with a narrow neck that can be
secured by a tie cord. Jab the bag all over with a thick sail
needle or meat skewer. Secure the bag to a rope, fill it with
oil and lower it over the windward side. If you don't have
a canvas bag and a supply of fish oil to hand, you can pierce
a metal oil-can with a small screwdriver, attach a line to the
handle and throw that over the side instead. Position the
bag or can so that the oil slick forms to windward.

NINE WAYS TO SAY HULL

English	*hull*
French	*coque*
German	*Rumpf*
Dutch	*romp*
Danish	*skrog*
Spanish	*casco*
Italian	*carena*
Portuguese	*casco*
Turkish	*karina*

CRUISING COCKTAILS

Pink Gin

There was a time when gin and Angostura bitters were essential items on board any yacht – especially if the skipper owned a blue blazer and a peaked cap. Those days are melting away like the ice that you may or may not place in your pink gin. Indeed, debate now rages about what exactly should go into this classic: some say water, some say tonic, some say nothing at all. There is one dark corner of the World Wide Web that substitutes grenadine for Angostura bitters – heaven forbid.

A proper cruising yachtsman's Pink Gin should be served thus:

1 Take a cracked plastic tumbler and wipe the rim with your shirt.
2 Add a good measure of gin. The amount will depend on whether the wake of a passing ferry jogs your arm at the vital moment – one can but hope.
3 Take what you hope is a bottle of Angostura Bitters (the label has peeled off and it could just be Tabasco or Lea & Perrins) and add a couple of splashes.

Serve without ice (real boats don't have freezers) the moment the mainsail cover has been put on.

ENSIGN ETIQUETTE

The ensign is the flag flown over the stern of a ship of yacht and is normally the national flag. The British red ensign contains the Union Flag in the top left corner of a red background and can be flown by all British yachts, registered or not. Under the Merchant Shipping Act all registered vessels are obliged to fly their ensigns when meeting other vessels, when entering or leaving foreign ports, or when approaching forts, signal and coastguard stations.

Members of the Royal Yacht Squadron may fly the white ensign while other selected organisations may fly the blue ensign or a defaced blue or red ensign.

It is considered good manners to fly your ensign in port during the official hours of daylight – these change around the world depending on the season. If an owner was giving up effective control of the vessel in the course of the day but people were remaining on board, it was deemed proper for the red and not a special ensign to be hoisted in the morning. The reason for this, given in the *Yachting World Handbook* of 1967, was that it was: 'considered demeaning to the status of ensigns to make exchanges of them during daylight'. Few people observe such niceties these days.

THAT'S DEEP MAN

The deepest waters in the world are to be found above the Mariana Trench in the Pacific Ocean. At 11,000 metres, or about seven miles, the odds of recovering a winch handle that slips over the side are slim.

The deepest point in the Atlantic Ocean is the Puerto Rico Trench at 8,648 metres (28,374 feet) while the deepest point of the Indian Ocean is the Java Trench, some 7,125 metres (23,376 feet) beneath the surface.

MIXED MESSAGES

The following conversation is alleged to have taken place between two radio operators – one American, one Canadian.

Canadian:	Please divert your course 15 degrees to the south to avoid a collision.
American:	Recommend you divert your course 15 degrees to the north to avoid a collision.
Canadian:	Negative. You will have to divert your course 15 degrees to the south to avoid a collision.
American:	This is the captain of a US navy ship. I say again, divert your course.
Canadian:	No. I say again, you divert your course.
American:	This is the aircraft carrier *USS Lincoln*, the second largest ship in the United States Atlantic fleet. We are accompanied by three destroyers, three cruisers and numerous support vessels. I demand that you change your course 15 degrees north – I say again, that's one-five degrees north – or counter-measures will be undertaken to ensure the safety of this ship.
Canadian:	This is a lighthouse. Your call.

NAUTICAL PUZZLES

The good ship *Saucy Sal* sets sail from Eastport, bound for Westport, 26 miles away. She sails the most direct route and makes a steady nine knots over the ground. At the same time the equally good ship *Naughty Nell* sets sail from Westport, bound for Eastport. She too sails in a straight line but makes only six knots. How long will it be before the two ships meet?

Answer on page 145

STUCK IN THE MUD

Running aground is as much a part of sailing as stubbing your toes and getting sunburnt. There are lots of ways to do it, but the preferred medium on which to ground is sand or mud – rock tends to be rather unforgiving.

Once aground you will want to refloat your vessel as quickly as possible. If the tide is rising you can just sit and wait to float off, but if it is ebbing you need to crack on. Firstly, try driving the boat backwards using the sails or engine. If this does not work you'll need to reduce the draught of the boat by heeling her over. Harden the sails in and ask the crew to stand amidships on one side. Still no joy? Lash some heavy objects (sail bags, jerry cans, in-laws) to the end of the boom and push it right out. In an extreme situation take a line from the top of the mast to the dinghy which should be motored or rowed at right angles to the lie of the yacht. This is unlikely to work but helps pass the time.

Rocking the boat from side to side may loosen the keel and allow you to slip away. This will take coordination among the crew who must rush from port to starboard and back again.

If you're stuck fast and the tide is ebbing away, then it may be time to think about survival. A rocky bottom could be fatal to your yacht's sides, so consider rigging the boom and spinnaker pole as legs to keep her upright. If you're drying out on a sandy bottom, things are a little less serious. Row out the anchor so that you won't float away when the tide comes in, then load the dinghy with heavy gear to lighten your craft. Inspect the ground for nasty rocks and shopping trolleys, and use bunk mattresses and sail bags to cushion the blow as your pride and joy settles on her sides.

If all else fails, don your wellies, hop over the side and start scrubbing the hull as though that was your intention all along!

MASTER AND COMMANDER

The Aubrey-Maturin novels of Patrick O'Brien capture the
essence of life at sea at the time of Napoleonic Wars and
sell in their millions. In chronological order they are:

Master and Commander • *Post Captain*
HMS Surprise • *The Mauritius Command*
Desolation Island • *The Fortune of War*
The Surgeon's Mate • *The Ionian Mission*
Treason's Harbour • *The Far Side of the World*
The Reverse of the Medal • *The Letter of Marque*
The Thirteen-Gun Salute • *The Nutmeg of Consolation*
The Truelove • *The Wine-Dark Sea*
The Commodore • *The Yellow Admiral*
The Hundred Days • *Blue at the Mizzen*

I THINK I'LL BUILD MY BOAT WITH...

Steel

Steel is heavy and hard. It is this latter characteristic that makes it popular with sailors who are venturing far from shore and friendly boatyards. There are many tales of steel yachts hitting rocks, ships, whales, containers and all other manner of hard hazards and surviving the encounter with only a dent or two.

Steel's great strength comes at a price – weight. A heavy boat can be a slow boat, but with the right rig she need not be, and heavier boats should be more stable and capable of pushing through large seas. Rust is steel's other downside. It is preventable, but only through regular and thorough maintenance – especially inside the boat. If you build or buy a steel boat expect to spend a lot of time with a paintbrush, as bare steel is rust's best friend. On the other hand you can be sure that wherever you go there will be someone with a welding kit to carry out any repairs.

SEA SAYINGS

Hunky dory

If everything is hunky dory you know there is nothing to worry about – although you might not realise exactly what you're saying. Sailors were certainly carefree when they visited Hunky-Dori, a street in Yokohama, Japan. Hunky-Dori was at the heart of the city's red light district and where every seaman's pleasure was catered for.

NOT IN MY SEA, YOU DON'T

It is generally accepted that a coastal state may exercise sovereignty over a belt of water adjacent to its coast. Most countries agree that this Territorial Sea cannot extend more than 12 miles from the coast. The Territorial Sea of the United Kingdom varies in width from three miles to the full 12 miles.

The Geneva Convention and United Nations Convention* allow vessels to pass through territorial waters if on innocent passage. This means they must not:

- Threaten or use force
- Exercise or practice with weapons
- Collect information (ie, spy)
- Take part in propaganda against the state
- Launch or land aircraft
- Load or unload people or commodities contrary to the laws of the coastal state
- Wilfully pollute
- Fish
- Carry out research or surveying activities
- Carry out any other activity not having direct bearing on the vessel's passage

*Not all maritime countries are parties to these conventions

71

INVENTIVE MEN AT SEA

William would have to redesign his pedalo many times before it became a commercial success.

HOW FAR?

The world's largest seas and oceans

		Sq kilometres	Sq miles
1	Pacific Ocean	166,242,500	64,186,600
2	Atlantic Ocean	86,557,800	33,420,160
3	Indian Ocean	73,427,800	28,350,640
4	Arctic Ocean	13,223,800	5,105,740
5	South China Sea	2,974,600	1,148,499
6	Caribbean Sea	2,515,900	971,400
7	Mediterranean Sea	2,510,000	969,120
8	Bering Sea	2,261,100	873,020
9	Sea of Okhotsk	1,527,570	589,800
10	Gulf of Mexico	1,507,600	582,100

The Pacific accounts for 46% of all the water on Earth, the Atlantic 23.9% and the Indian Ocean 20.3%.

Sailors share the seas with all types of craft, and one of the biggest of them all is *Hellesport Fairfax*, or just *Fairfax* to her friends. When it comes to moving oil by sea, economies of scale mean that building big boats makes sense and *Fairfax* is a monster.

Built in South Korea, she is longer than six jumbo jets parked nose to tail and her rudder is bigger than a tennis court. She cost a whopping $65 million, but such is the demand for shipping oil from the Middle East to the US that she covered her building costs after just six trips. *Fairfax* can carry 3.2 million barrels of oil in 21 separate tanks, allowing her to transport several different grades of crude oil at a time. Each tank is bigger than an Olympic-size swimming pool. After the oil is pumped out, robotic showerheads descend into the tanks, cleaning them of any residue and readying them for the next load.

Fairfax is too big to pass through the Suez Canal, so has to take the long way round from Saudi Arabia to the US via the Cape of Good Hope at the southern tip of Africa. So if you're down that way and running low on oil, you may be lucky and come across the *Hellesport Fairfax*, which should be able to spare you a gallon or two.

RANKS OF ENLISTED SAILORS IN THE ROYAL NAVY

Warrant Officer
Chief Petty Officer
Petty Officer
Leading Seaman
Able Seaman
Ordinary Seaman

ROCK LIGHTHOUSES OF BRITAIN

These marvels of engineering have been constructed in
these most testing of locations to keep mariners safe

Eddystone, *Devon*
The Skerries, *Wales*
The Smalls, *Wales*
Longships, *Cornwall*
The Longstone, *Northumberland*
Bell Rock, *Scotland*
Skerryvore, *Scotland*
Bishop Rock, *Isles of Scilly*
Wolf Rock, *Cornwall*
Dubh Artach, *Scotland*
Chicken Rock, *Isle of Man*
Flannan Isles, *Scotland*

HOW TO ABANDON SHIP

Yachtsmen are told they should only step up into a life raft. This advice should not be taken literally, but it is true that a yacht should generally not be abandoned until she is definitely sinking. A damaged yacht offers more shelter than a life raft, is more stable and is easier for rescuers to locate. If you are forced into it, a life raft will contain some safety equipment but, if time allows, take as much food, clothing and emergency supplies as is practical. Lash your dinghy to your life raft and use it to carry extra stores. Fill any suitable containers about three-quarters full with fresh water, so that they will float. If you need glasses to read instructions (on flares, etc) have a spare pair in an emergency grab bag, along with vital medication and paperwork. You should also include navigational gear, emergency beacons and transponders, and handheld VHFs.

GOING DOWN

Boats are generally not designed to sink, but there are a few that make their living by doing exactly that. Biggest of them all is *Mighty Servant*, which her owners claim to be the strongest ship on the planet.

Mighty Servant earns her keep by carrying huge structures, such as oilrigs, across the world's oceans. Her cargo deck is 150m long and 50m wide and capable of carrying cargo weighing 45,000 tonnes. There is not a crane on the planet that could lift such a weight, so how does *Mighty Servant* get her cargo on board? By sinking.

This remarkable vessel has seacocks that can be opened, flooding ballast tanks with 70,000 tonnes of seawater. The accommodation section and bridge stay above the waves while the cargo deck sinks 22m below. Oilrigs and other giant, floating cargo can then be manoeuvred over the deck and held in place by tugs while *Mighty Servant* pumps out the ballast and slowly rises, lifting the cargo clear of the water. Piggyback, anyone?

SAILING TERMS THAT
CONFUSE LANDLUBBERS

Knot

A knot is a knot, except at sea when it's not. Though it can be. Refer to a knot at sea and the sea dogs on board will presume you are talking about a measure of speed – one nautical mile per hour, to be precise. At sea the thing you make by tying a rope around itself or another rope is called by a specific name, such as a figure of eight or bowline. Ironically the original meaning of 'knot' became a victim of its own success. To work out a vessel's speed, a piece of wood was thrown overboard with a line attached. Knots were tied in the line at regular intervals and the rate with which they passed allowed you to calculate your speed. Knot a lot of people know that.

THE MEDITERRANEAN MOOR

Not to be confused with Othello, the Moor of Venice, the Mediterranean moor is also complex and consists of different acts. There are relatively few marina berths or floating moorings in the Med and it is usual to moor your boat with her stern against the quayside, allowing you to step off the stern and into the nearest bar. Securing the back of the boat is easy; the tricky part is keeping the bows pointing out to sea. This is done by dropping the anchor as you approach the dockside in reverse. It's best to start reversing a long way out so that you have good control of the boat and can straighten up for the final approach. When about four boat-lengths from the quay, give the order to drop the anchor. Your crew must pay out the chain quickly to allow the yacht to continue its smooth backwards progress. Slowly approach the quay and give a blip of forward power at the last minute to stop the boat. A fender slung over the stern is a wise precaution. Lines are attached from the stern to the quay and the anchor chain can now be slowly hauled in to stop the bow swinging about.

It takes a little practice to master the Mediterranean moor and the fact that you are providing the entertainment for all the diners in the quayside tavernas does little to help the novice's nerves.

POINTS OF SAIL

The angle at which a boat is heading, relative to the direction of the wind, is known as the point of sail. There are five principal points of sail, from facing directly into the wind to having it dead astern.

Head-to-wind • Close-hauled
Close reach • Beam reach
Broad reach • Run

FLARES ARE BACK IN

The following flares must be carried onboard to
comply with Royal Ocean Racing Club rules:
Four red parachute
Two orange floating
Four red pinpoint
Four white collision

STEADY AS A ... SHIP

Sailors go to sea for pleasure, and if they spend the voyage
with their head over the side 'feeding the fishes', then they
have no one to blame but themselves. Those for whom the
sea is simply a place where they work can be more resent-
ful of the motion of the ocean – especially if it stops them
from getting on with their jobs. Scientists need a steady
base from which to work more than most, so those fortu-
nate enough to work on the *Kilo Moana* have no cause for
complaint. Meaning 'One who seeks to understand the
sea', *Kilo Moana* is a research vessel that spends long peri-
ods of time in the roughest parts of the North Pacific where
the scientists that she carries study climate change.

Kilo Moana is a catamaran and maintains her steady foot-
ing among the shifting seas due to two torpedo-like pon-
toons that lie at the foot of each hull. These giant structures provide the buoyancy to lift the rest of the vessel
above the breaking seas yet are deep enough not to be troubled by the rise and fall of the ocean swell. The sections of
each hull that link the torpedoes to the superstructure are
incredibly thin, offering the minimum of resistance to the
waves and thus allowing the *Kilo Moana* to stay remark-
ably balanced. The technology is still in its infancy, but
who knows, perhaps the day is not too far away when
everyone who goes to sea will be sailing on an even keel.

THE REALITY OF SAILING

Electronics

Electronics make a sailor's life easier. At least that's the theory. In practice you go into a chandlery to be blinded by science and pay hundreds of pounds for a bit of kit that will be out of date in six months. Having got it on board, you realise that you'll have to drill dozens of holes in your bulkheads to mount the thing and all the wires are in the wrong place to connect it to your other kit. You run your engine for an hour to get enough power to start it (your other electronics have flattened your battery) and then attack the instructions booklet. The 'plug and play' promise does not come instantly true and you start to curse whoever translated the manual from Korean. You begin to get the hang of your kit but discover that it's not talking to your other onboard gizmos, which makes it virtually redundant. Your phone the helpline (calls are charged at £1.50 per minute) and eventually are told that you need to buy an extra cable that costs £20. You return to the chandlery, buy the cable, get back to the boat and plug it in. Everything works. You're ecstatic until you realise that the wind has died, the tide's gone out and it's started raining. You call it a day and head for home, wishing that you had gone sailing instead.

NAUTICAL PUZZLES

You need to make a new mast for your yacht and see a perfectly shaped tree trunk sticking out of the riverbed. You know that one-half of the pole is in the ground, another one-third of it is covered by water, and 11ft is out of the water.
What is the total length of the pole in feet?
Answer on page 145

NAUTICAL PHOBIAS

Irrational fears that may keep you away from the water

Ablutophobia	Fear of washing
Ancraophobia	Fear of wind
Bathophobia	Fear of depth
Bromidrosiphobia	Fear of body smells
Cymophobia	Fear of sea swell
Erythrophobia	Fear of port-hand markers
Homichlophobia	Fear of fog
Hydrophobia	Fear of the sea
Hygrophobia	Fear of dampness
Ichthyophobia	Fear of fish
Limnophobia	Fear of lakes
Potamophobia	Fear of rivers
Thalassophobia	Fear of the sea

NOXIOUS LIQUID SUBSTANCES

Merchant shipping regulations identify four types of Noxious Liquid Substances (NLS). Discharges of them into the sea are prohibited.

Category A
Present a major hazard to either marine resources or human health and justify the application of stringent antipollution measures

Category C
Present a minor hazard to either marine resources or human health and require special operational conditions

Category B
Present a hazard to either marine resources or human health and justify the application of special anti-pollution measures

Category D
Present a major hazard to either marine resources or human health and require some attention in operational conditions

A NAUTICAL JOKE

A sailor meets a pirate in a bar. The pirate has a peg leg, a hook and an eye patch. 'How'd you end up with a peg leg?' asks the sailor. 'I was swept overboard in a storm,' says the pirate. 'A shark bit off me whole leg.' 'Wow!' says the sailor. 'What about the hook?' 'We were boarding an enemy ship, battling the other seamen with swords. One of them cut me hand clean off.' 'Incredible!' remarks the sailor. 'And the eye patch?' 'A seagull dropping fell in me eye,' replies the pirate. 'You lost your eye to a seagull dropping?' the sailor asks incredulously. The pirate shrugs and replies: 'It was me first day with the hook.'

PORT AND STARBOARD

Left and right will suffice for the man in the street, but at sea it must always be port and starboard. The word 'port', to mean 'left', is a relatively recent innovation, and the British and US navies only officially took it onboard in the nineteenth century. Prior to this, the opposite to 'starboard' was 'larboard', but the similarity between the two words meant that port got its big break.

The port side of any vessel will show a red light at night, while green lights are displayed to starboard. This helps you work out what other shipping is doing after the sun goes down, and is vital to avoid collisions.

If you have problems remembering that port is left and that red lights are shown on that side of a vessel, try to recall Mr Red who left port, or consider the fact that port is red and there is none left in the bottle. But don't feel bad if you can't remember – there are plenty of tales of captains of giant liners and admirals of aircraft carriers carrying slips of paper in their pockets on which are written simply: Port – left. Starboard – right.

Prior to the invention of modern foot pumps, small whales were often used to inflate rubber dinghies.

A STAR TO GUIDE ME

Some of the stars visible in the northern hemisphere that are used for traditional navigation

Altair • Ddeneb • Mirfak
Aldeebaran • Rigel
Bellatrix • Alnilam • Elnath
Capella • Procyon
Arcturus • Vega • Alkaid
Alioth • Spica • Regulus
Dubhe • Rasalhague

ANOTHER KIND OF SEAGULL

A Seagull outboard was once the engine of choice of any self-respecting sailor. Clamped to their dinghy, it would be used to propel them, quickly and efficiently, to their yacht. At least that was the idea. The reality was slightly different.

There now exists a generation of yachtsmen who know only the neat, light, clean and reliable Japanese and Korean outboards. Seagulls, like their feathered namesakes, were noisy and could be very messy. No quick pull of a chord to get this engine going – starting a Seagull involves a complex ritual passed down from father to son.

First a pull cord must be made from a bit of old rope with a knot in the end. This rope is wound round the drum atop the engine. Then the fuel: a twist of the air valve on the fuel tank, a fiddle in the engine's bowels to open the fuel tap; a tickle of the tickler to draw fuel into the chamber; a wiggle of the choke depending on the weather, state of tide and level of optimism. The throttle is adjusted and the chord can finally be pulled.

Anyone sitting in the dinghy must be warned of the imminent start. This gives them the chance to turn their backs to the mighty Seagull and cower – hopefully keeping their vital organs out of harm's way.

The starter (generally the strongest person on board) then makes sure the drum is wound tight and gives an almighty heave. If he falls over and the engine fails to start (which is usually the case), he clambers to his feet and starts the whole process again. Perhaps a little less choke this time and a touch more throttle. Wind up the drum. Warn crew. Pull!

If Neptune is smiling, the Seagull will roar into life and you'll be on your way. Until the propeller becomes fouled with weed, that is. To clear it, the engine is tipped forward so the spinning propeller throws water and weed over everyone.

They just don't make 'em like that any more.

WHICH WAY'S UP?

Nothing at sea is a simple as it first appears. Take directions for example: as well as port and starboard replacing left and right there's also leeward (away from the wind) and windward (towards it). Port and starboard are relative to the direction of the vessel, while leeward and windward depend on the direction of the wind. At least compass directions remain constant and simple – if only.

Direction can be referenced to three different Norths and if you confuse them you could easily find yourself on the rocks. True North is measured from the Geographic North Pole – the place where explorers stick flags. Magnetic North is measured from the Magnetic North Pole – which doesn't coincide with the Geographic North and can move about. Compass North is wherever the end of the compass needle says it is. This can be affected by all manner of metallic and electrical objects on board. Charts usually show True North, but bearings and tracks calculated from this must be converted to Magnetic before being used to steer by.

CRUISING COCKTAILS

Sex on the Beach

This cocktail is well named, as, like the real thing, it sounds like a good idea at the time but can leave you sore in the morning if you overindulge.

Take a long glass (or an old orange mug if you are on a gaff-rigged yacht) and throw in some ice if you have it. Add a healthy tot of vodka and an equal quantity of peach schnapps. Top up with fresh orange juice and cranberry juice – watch out for the pips. A couple of crushed raspberries finishes it all off. Rinse everything well afterwards to clean off any seeds that have not been swallowed.

SNUFF'S ENOUGH

There were fortunes to be made at sea during the seventeenth and eighteenth centuries, and naval warfare and piracy were both constants. Victory was normally decided by the skill with which a ship was handled, the direction of the wind or the strength of a ship's firepower – however, in 1702, a naval engagement was decided by a cargo of snuff.

The English Navy was attacking the French and Spanish fleets, and things didn't look good for one of the English ships that had been set on fire by a enemy fireship. Fortunately the fireship had a cargo of snuff which blew up with such force that the blast extinguished the flames onboard the English vessel. A witness recorded that: 'It so affected the crews of the French warships that many of them had to dive into the sea for relief from the pain of having inhaled the snuff.'

TIME FOR A NAP?

If there's one thing you need a lot of when single-handing a 60ft racing yacht around the world, it's sleep. However, with your competitors pushing their boats hard, there's no respite – take your foot off the gas, so to speak, and you'll be passed. If you're asleep, you aren't getting the most from your boat and reacting to every wind shift and wave.

If this is your problem, take a tip from Ellen MacArthur, Britain's leading single-handed yachtswoman. When she set off round the world in the Vendée Globe in 2000, she knew that she had to sleep as little as possible yet still be mentally and physically fit enough to cope with the challenges that the oceans would throw at her. Her solution was to catch snatches of sleep at intervals throughout the day. During her 94-day voyage she slept 891 times – but her average time asleep was just 36 minutes.

INTERNATIONAL FLAG CODES

There is a different flag for every letter in the alphabet, and each, when flown alone, has a specific meaning:

A Diver below (when stationary); I am undergoing a speed trial
B I am taking on or discharging explosives
C Yes (affirmative)
D Keep clear of me, I am manoeuvring with difficulty
E I am altering my course to starboard
F I am disabled, communicate with me
G I require a pilot
H I have a pilot on board
I I am altering my course to port
J I am going to send a message by semaphore
K You should stop your vessel instantly
L You should stop, I have something important to communicate
M I have a doctor on board
N No (negative)
O Man overboard
P The Blue Peter – all aboard, vessel is about to proceed to sea. At sea: your lights are out or burning badly
Q My vessel is healthy and I request free practique (permission to travel freely)
R The way is off my ship (I am not moving). You may feel your way past me
S My engines are going full speed astern
T Do not pass ahead of me
U You are standing (moving) into danger
V I require assistance (not distress)
W I require medical assistance
X Stop carrying out your intentions and watch for my signals
Y I am carrying mail
Z To be used to address or call shore stations

SEA SAYINGS

Slush fund

Ship's cooks supplemented their meagre pay by selling the fat from salted meat storage barrels. This slush, valued by candle makers, provided cooks with valuable extra income.

HOW TO FILLET A MACKEREL

No fish are easier to catch from a sailing boat than mackerel. Nearly every yacht has a mackerel line with spinners or feathered hooks to snare these most British of fish. Simply unwind the line from the stern, make sure you don't sail too fast, wait for 10 minutes and reel in the line. Repeat until you get lucky – it rarely takes long.

Once you have the fish on board, you'll need to kill them. Different people adopt different techniques, but a quick blow to the head with a winch handle often does the trick. Once dead, the head can be cut off and the fish gutted. To do this, insert a knife in the bottom of the fish near the tail, and draw forwards. Scoop everything out from the cavity you have revealed and rinse the mackerel.

You are now faced with two choices: cooking or eating raw. The latter option may not be immediately appealing, but you will rarely be able to eat sushi as fresh as this. If you don't have soy sauce, wasabi and pickled ginger to hand, you may decide to cook the fish. A knob of butter in a frying pan is all you need, but you can easily fillet the fish first by running a knife along the spine from tail to head. Smoking your fillets is a delicious alternative to frying them. Portable fish smokers can be bought for about £50 and, armed with methylated spirit to create the heat and sawdust to make the smoke, you can make smoked mackerel fillets in a matter of minutes that taste infinitely better than the shrink-wrapped versions sold in supermarkets.

TWINKLE, TWINKLE

There are few experiences as magical as sailing through a sea that is alight with phosphorescence. This most remarkable of natural phenomena is caused by biochemical reactions in a variety of sea creatures. Some fish can turn their lights on and off, drawing prey to them or scaring attackers away, however, the lights most commonly seen when sailing come from tiny animals and occur when the water is disturbed by waves or a yacht's wake. A dolphin swimming in such waters becomes an illuminated torpedo or an underwater firework. Such 'disturbed water luminescence' is sometimes seen around British shores but is more common in warmer climates and is not the only type of phosphorescence. Parts of the Arabian Sea can give off a constant, even white glow known as the Milky Sea. Sailors throughout the years have described beams of light moving quickly over the waters of the Indian Ocean and the China Sea and official Admiralty publications include descriptions of 'luminous masses apparently coming to the surface and exploding' to light up a large area, as well as flashing patches and areas of light that apparently expand and contract.

EMERGENCY SUPPLIES

What you can expect to find in a typical offshore life raft

Oars • Bailer • Repair kit
Flashlight • Spare batteries
Jack knife • Flares, handheld
Hand pump • Water packets
Rations • Water storage bag
Fishing kit • Sponge • Signal mirror
First aid kit • Seasickness tablets
Survival manual • SOLAS parachute flare

SEAGULLS

Seagulls sometimes like to dry their little seagull bottoms and have a bit of a waddle after a swim. Unfortunately they do not confine their waddling to the seashore or the local council tip, but also settle on yachts' decks – and seagulls are not fussy about where they go to the loo. Leave your boat for a couple of weeks and you will probably return to find her decks encrusted in guano, which takes an age to scrub away.

Sailors spend a lot of time and money keeping seagulls and their droppings off their decks. Some tie carrier bags on pieces of string from the boom, these flutter in the wind and look horrible to seagulls and other yachtsmen. Others laboriously crisscross their decks with tape, preventing the birds from settling at all. CDs are hung from the rigging of some yachts, though whether seagulls are more averse to Barry Manilow than Britney Spears is not yet known. If things get desperate you can buy a bird scarer that will either go bang every few minutes, or replicate the sound of a hungry hawk about to descend from the skies for a seagull snack. Neither audible option is likely to prove popular with neighbouring yachts. Keeping a fox, ferret or cat on board does work, though there are animal cruelty issues involved, so make your choice carefully.

SEA SAYINGS

Toe the line

One explanation of this everyday saying is that when a ship's crew were ordered to 'fall in' they would line up on deck. To ensure a neat alignment of each row, the sailors were directed to stand with their toes just touching a particular seam between a pair of planks. Anyone who disobeyed was told to 'toe the line'.

FAMOUS WATERY DEATHS

People who should have stayed away from boats – or water in general

Donald Crowhurst
Famous yachtsman, said to have 'stepped overboard'

Harold Holt
Australian PM, drowned

Lord Lucan
Alleged murderer, presumed drowned mid-Channel

Kirsty MacColl
Pop star, killed in a jet ski accident

Robert Maxwell
Media mogul, drowned after falling overboard

Percy Shelley *Poet,* drowned while sailing off Italy

Natalie Wood *Actress,* fell overboard while securing the tender

Virginia Woolf *Author,* drowned in the River Ouse

I THINK I'LL BUILD MY BOAT WITH...

Glass Reinforced Plastic

Glass Reinforced Plastic, or GRP, revolutionised the boat building industry in the 1960s and 1970s. The vast majority of modern yachts are built from this strong, versatile, cheap and easily shaped material. GRP's greatest attraction is the fact that it more or less looks after itself. Unlike wood it will not rot, and unlike steel it will not rust, though it does not have the same ability to withstand knocks as some other materials.

Osmosis, or the dreaded boat pox, is GRP's Achilles' heel. Air spaces in the hull draw in water, causing the holes to grow bigger, weakening the structure of the boat. It is a problem in some older boats but is now rare and many yachts that used to suffer have been successfully treated. If you don't have a huge amount of time or money and don't plan to voyage far from a boatyard, then GRP is almost certainly for you.

ALL AT SEA

'Strewth captain! Look at that for a poor bit of parking.'

TRAFFIC LIGHTS

Confined entrances to ports and harbours are sometimes controlled by a system of traffic lights, which are usually three vertical lights.

Three red flashing	Serious emergency: stop or divert
Three red	Do not proceed
Three green	Proceed, one-way traffic
Top two green	Proceed, two-way traffic
Top and bottom green	Proceed only when instructed

RACING FOR PLEASURE

Sailors have always tried to sail their boats as fast as possible. For many years the drive behind this need for speed was purely commercial – the sooner you reached the fishing grounds or trading port, the sooner you could catch your fish or sell your cargo.

But men are naturally competitive and wherever there are two similar sailing boats, there is likely to be some sort of race taking place. The first documented race of modern times took place in 1661 when King Charles raced his brother, the Duke of York, on a course from Greenwich to Gravesend. The King won and yacht racing has never looked back since.

CRUISING COCKTAILS

Rum Punch

When in Rome do as the Romans, and when sailing in the Caribbean, drink rum punch. For the yachtsman, no drink is as closely linked to a place as is rum punch and the clear blue seas and fresh winds of the Caribbean.

There are as many ways to make this classic cocktail as there are delightful anchorages and sleepy ports, and as long as it tastes great and gets you dancing, no one will complain. If in doubt, stick to this basic formula:

> One of sour
> Two of sweet
> Three of strong
> And four of weak

The sour is normally lime juice, though some add bitters too. The sweet is sugar syrup, but pineapple and orange juice often appear. The strong has to be rum, of which there is rarely a shortage, and the weak can be anything from water to more juice.

THE AULD MUG

The America's Cup, dating from 1851, is considered by some to be the oldest trophy in international sport. No prize money is awarded to the winner, yet racing syndicates spend tens of millions of dollars mounting campaigns to either defend or challenge for the America's Cup and prove their technological supremacy at sea.

The cup itself, known as the Auld Mug, is 26 inches tall and made from 134 ounces of silver-plated Britannia metal (similar to pewter). It was crafted by R&G Garrard, Queen's jewellers, in London, in about 1848. The cup was made for the Royal Yacht Squadron as a yacht racing trophy and was originally dubbed the 100 Guinea Cup. A seven-inch base was added to the America's Cup in 1958 to accommodate the additional winners' names.

BEYOND THE HORIZON

Excitement and adventure always lie beyond the horizon, but just how far is that? Well it all depends how tall you are and how far above sea level you are standing. The rough rule is to increase the square root of the number of feet that the eye is above sea level by one third of itself. The result will be the distance of the horizon in miles. If that seems like hard work you can use this table:

Height above sea level (feet)	Distance to horizon (miles)
5	2.9
20	5.9
50	9.3
100	13.2
500	29.5
1,000	41.6
2,000	58.9
5,000	93.1

THE OLDEST YACHT CLUBS
IN THE WORLD

Flotilla of the Neva, Russia, *1718*
Royal Cork Yacht Club, Ireland, *1720*
Lough Ree Yacht Club, Ireland, *1770*
Starcross Yacht Club, UK, *1772*
Royal Thames Yacht Club, England, UK, *1775*
Royal Yacht Squadron, UK, *1815*
Republic of Singapore Yacht Club, Singapore, *1826*
Royal Western Yacht Club of England, UK, *1827*
Royal Swedish Yacht Club, Sweden, *1830*
Royal Irish Yacht Club, Ireland, *1831*
Lough Derg Yacht Club, Ireland, *1835*
Royal Eastern Yacht Club, UK, *1835–1969*
Royal Malta Yacht Club, Malta, *1835*
Royal Nova Scotia Yacht Squadron, Canada, *1837*
Royal Southern Yacht Club, UK, *1837*
Tamar Yacht Club, Australia, *1837*
Deben Yacht Club, UK, *1838*
Royal St George Yacht Club, Ireland, *1838*
Royal Perth Yacht Club, Australia, *1841*
Societé des Retates du Havre, France, *1842*
Royal Harwich Yacht Club, UK, *1843*
Royal Bermuda Yacht Club, Bermuda, *1844*
Royal Victoria Yacht Club, UK, *1845*
Royal Bombay Yacht Club, India, *1846*
Royal Netherlands Yacht Club, The Netherlands, *1847*
Royal Row & Sailing Society, *1851*
Poole Yacht Club, UK, *1852*
Royal Canadian Yacht Club, Canada, *1852*
Royal Yacht Club of Victoria, Australia, *1853*
Goolwa Regatta Yacht Club, Australia, *1854*
Associacao Naval de Lisboa, Portugal *1856*
Ranelagh Yacht Club, UK, *c.1857*
Royal Temple Yacht Club, UK *1857*
Royal Natal Yacht Club, South Africa *1858*

WARM AND DRY

A generation of sailors is emerging that does not know what it is like to be really wet and cold. Their ignorance of these twin miseries is a result of the massive improvements made to sailing clothing. Whatever sort of boat you sail, and wherever you sail her, you will be warmer and drier than yachtsmen of yesteryear ever thought possible.

If you are more than 30 years old, you are likely to recall your dinghy sailing days: Peter Storm oilskins that crackled as you walked worn over a pair of jeans and a big jumper, plimsolls on your feet and a massive orange Crewsaver lifejacket on top of it all. Today's dinghy sailor will wear a wet suit, or even a dry suit, with neoprene boots and a slim buoyancy aid.

When they graduate to yachts, today's sailor will experience the joys of the layering system: a snug base layer, a fleece-lined mid layer and a totally waterproof top layer. All of it will be breathable to let the sweat out without letting the sea in. His boots will be breathable too and he will laugh at the thought of the yachtsman of old in his plastic boots and yellow sou'wester.

KNOT ANOTHER BOAT NAME

Knot To Worry	Knot 4 Sail
Knot Tonight	Knot for Long
Knot Yours	Knot Home
Knot Wise	Knot Shore
Knot-A-Wake	Knot Me
Knot-on-Call	Knot on Duty
Knot Again	Knot Bad
Knot a Care	Knot So Fast
Knot a Yacht	Knot Paid For
Knot Bored	Knot Now

WINTER CHECKLIST

Taking your boat out of the water for the winter?
Don't forget to:

Clean fuel filters
Change the oil
Add antifreeze to coolants
Remove the impeller
Coat battery terminals in Vaseline
Take all sails down
Secure halyards
Ventilate the boat
Clean the heads
Grease the seacocks
Check for osmosis

– and make a note of all the jobs you've done so you
don't do them again in the spring.

SCURVY

For 300 years, up to 1800, more seafarers died for want of
a lemon than for any other reason. Scurvy, a disease caused
by a deficiency of vitamin C (ascorbic acid), causes spongy,
bleeding gums, hard patches on the skin, weakness and,
ultimately, death. It is easily cured by a diet containing
fresh fruit and vegetables and is unlikely to arise before six
weeks of dietary neglect. Captain Cook ensured his men
had a varied diet and thus kept scurvy at bay, but he did
not recognise the crucial role of vitamin C. In 1753 scien-
tist James Lind published a treatise urging the Navy to
issue lemon juice as a preventative. Forty years later they
took his advice and scurvy was wiped out. It did, however,
reappear a few decades later when limes were substituted
for lemons. Their lower levels of ascorbic acid failed to
prevent scurvy but gave Britons the name 'Limeys'.

SHIP IN DISTRESS

A few distress signals that may be heard or seen at sea

- A gun or other explosive device fired at intervals of about a minute.
- Continuous sounding of any fog-signal apparatus.
- Rockets or shells, throwing red stars, fired one at a time, at short intervals.
- A signal made by radiotelephony or by any other signalling method consisting of the group - - - — — — - - - ('SOS' in Morse code).
- A signal sent by radiotelephony consisting of the spoken word 'mayday'.
- The international code of signals (normally flags) for distress indicated by 'NC'.
- A signal consisting of a square flag having above or below it a ball, or anything resembling a ball.
- Flames on the vessel (as from a burning tar barrel, oil barrel, etc).
- Rocket parachute flare or hand flare showing a red light.
- A smoke signal giving off orange-coloured smoke.
- Slowly and repeatedly raising and lowering arms outstretched to each side.
- The radiotelegraph alarm signal (12 four-second dashes per minute set at one-second intervals).
- The radiotelephone alarm signal (alternate tones of 1300Hz and 220Hz transmitted on 2182kHz for a period of 30 to 60 seconds).
- Signals transmitted by Emergency Position-Indicating Radio Beacons (EPIRBs).
- Approved signals transmitted by radio communications systems, allowing the full range of marine distress equipment to be employed.
- Standing naked in a life raft in the middle of the Pacific Ocean, shouting 'Help!' and waving your arms madly. (Unofficial, but effective.)

UNIDENTIFIED FLOATING OBJECTS

While oilrigs can be a hazard to sailors, rising up out of the sea, at least they are anchored to the seabed. The same cannot be said of semi-submersible rigs – huge mobile structures propel themselves across the oceans, searching for oil and gas. The biggest of these is *Eric Raude*, named after Viking Eric the Red. For $150,000 a day you can charter *Eric* to comb the North Atlantic, searching for the estimated 78 trillion cubic feet of gas that are believed to lie there.

Eric is propelled by Rolls-Royce thrusters, the biggest ever built, which are linked to satellite navigation systems. When she is over the drill spot, the thrusters constantly balance her position to counter wind, waves and currents. When the drilling is finished they can swivel to face in the same direction and drive the rig through the sea to her next destination.

Eric was built to cope with conditions in what her captain describes as 'the meanest, roughest, toughest place to work'. North Atlantic storms are some of the most ferocious on the planet, as proved by the loss of the semi-submersible *Ocean Ranger* in a storm prior to *Eric*'s launch. No one survived that tragedy, which caused designers to rethink how semi-submersibles should be built. Eric has subsequently made it through three 'hundred-year storms' – the sort that normally come only once a century – and her crew have now grown to trust her.

CRUISING COCKTAILS

Harbour Lights

Always a welcome sight at the end of a long day on the water. Pour a couple of fingers of vodka into a glass. Add four fingers of peach juice (in emergency use the syrup from one of those cans you've got at the back of a locker). Top up with cranberry juice and a splash of lemonade.

THE FASTNET RACE

In 1925, 14 yachts raced from the Solent, down the English Channel and around the Fastnet Rock off Ireland, ending up in Plymouth. There was debate at the time as to whether such an Ocean Race (as it was known) was a safe and sensible thing to do. That first race was won by Jolie Brise in six days and three hours, and the event soon became a famous fixture in the yachting calendar.

Fame turned to infamy in 1979 when the fleet of the Fastnet race was caught in storm in the Atlantic. The racing yachts of the day simply could not cope with the terrible conditions. Of the 303 yachts that started the race, 23 were abandoned or sunk. Of the 2,500 sailors who took part, 136 were rescued and 15 died. The race is still held every year but the Fastnet disaster has had a huge impact on the design of ocean-going boats, and the quantity and design of safety equipment they must now carry.

TEN TYPES OF ICE

Anchor ice	Submerged ice attached or anchored to the bottom
Bare ice	Ice without snow cover
Brash ice	Accumulations of ice made up of fragments not more than 2m across
Compact ice	No water is visible
Fast ice	Sea ice that forms and remains fast along the coast
Firn	Old snow that is not as dense as ice
Floe	A flat piece of ice 20m or more across
Ice cake	A flat piece of ice less than 20m across
Nunatak	Rocky outcrop projecting from and surrounded by a glacier or ice sheet
Thaw holes	Vertical holes in sea ice

THE EARLY YEARS OF THE RNLI

1824   Sir William Hillary, a courageous lifeboatman, coordinates the first lifeboat service. His appeal to the nation leads to the foundation of the National Institution for the Preservation of Life from Shipwreck, later to become the RNLI. The same year the Gold Medal for outstanding bravery is founded.

1830   Sir William Hillary receives a Gold Medal for his part in the rescue of the crew of the St George.

1839   The number of lifeboat stations around Britain reaches 30.

1840   Early rescues are made using the Manby rocket.

1843   The 50th dedicated lifeboat is launched in Cromer.

1849   Lives saved total 6,716.

1854   Captain Ward, an RNLI Inspector, invents a cork lifejacket, which gives lifeboat crews weather protection as well as buoyancy.

1854   The Institution changes its name to the Royal National Lifeboat Institution.

SAILING TERMS THAT
CONFUSE LANDLUBBERS

Clew

Tell your skipper that you haven't a clue and he'll probably agree. Tell him that you haven't a clew and he'll tell you to bloody well find one and tie a rope to it. The clew is the outside bottom (or 'aft lower', in sailing speak) corner of a sail, to which is attached the sheets that control the sail. The sheets are ropes that run through blocks, though the blocks are not blocks at all. Instead of being square, as a block should be, they are mostly round, to allow ropes to pass smoothly through them, and are used to lead the sheets towards the stern – but don't let the name fool you, some sterns can be very jolly places.

WHAT A SUPERYACHT

There are yachts and then there are superyachts. There is no precise way of defining whether you are looking at a big yacht or a superyacht, except that if you need to ask the question then it's not a superyacht. These boats are used by the rich and famous as mobile apartments and luxury playthings. They are kept in the Mediterranean for the summer then taken to the Caribbean to cruise under the winter sun.

Superyachts need not have sails, though more and more luxury craft are being built that combine opulence with some of the style that can only come with a boat that can be driven by sail alone. These vessels are incredibly expensive to build and their super-rich owners are often too busy either making money or spending it to make much use of them. So they remain on standby, kept perpetually polished for the day the owner's Ferrari roars into the marina.

If you lack the millions but fancy the lifestyle, why not sign up as crew on a superyacht? The hours can be long and the owners can be demanding but you get to sail the world in luxury and will have the boat to yourself for long stretches. You can play with the toys onboard – jet-skis, windsurfers, etc – and don't have to pay any tax on your generous salary.

If this sounds like the life for you, it's best to get as many sailing or motorboat qualifications as possible before heading to the sun, doing the rounds of the marinas and hoping your boat comes in.

NAUTICAL PUZZLES

Rearrange this phrase to discover a nautical command:
Headlands clonk
Answer on page 145

A SEAFARING NATION

'You couldn't have a look at my rudder mounting while you're down there?' King Arthur asked tentatively.

SEA SINGERS

Bands with a nautical sound

The Beach Boys • Bow Wow Wow
Creedence Clearwater Revival
Flock of Seagulls • Katrina and the Waves
The Lighthouse Family
Ocean Colour Scene • Sailor
The Seahorses • Starsailor
The Waterboys

LASER POWER

When it first appeared in 1969, the Laser dinghy revolutionised dinghy sailing, and it is still going strong. Although more than 30 years old, it is still the dinghy of choice for many sailors, combining simplicity and speed. More than 100,000 have been built and there are competitive fleets of them in every corner of the world. The Laser is an Olympic class dinghy and with its 76 square feet of sail can be a demanding boat to sail. Fortunately the original Laser now has numerous brothers and sisters allowing all sorts of people to enjoy Laser sailing.

Laser	Single-handed adult
Laser Radial	Single-handed small adult, women and youth
Laser 4.7	Single-handed small youth
Laser Pico	One adult/two adults/adult-child/two or three children
Laser Funboat	One adult/adult-child/two children
Laser 2 Regatta	Two-person adult racing
Laser Vortex	Single-handed adult
Laser 2000	Two adult – two adult/two children
Laser 4000	Two-person adult racing
Laser Stratos	For all the family
Laser SB3	3 person adult

WHAT'S IN A NAME

Celebs who sound as if they should be at sea...

Brian Ferry • Rod Hull
Roger Moore • Billy Ocean
Diana Rigg • David Seaman
Sandy Shaw • Howard Stern
Pete Waterman

THREE PEAKS

There is something slightly masochistic about going sailing. Unless you are on a luxury liner, there will be certain privations that must be endured when at sea. Some tolerate these little hardships, others enjoy them but some people still find the whole thing still too easy. It was for these people that Bill Tilman devised the Three Peaks Race.

Tilman was a mountaineer and yachtsman and the race reflects his twin passions. Yachts starts at Barmouth in mid-Wales and sail 62 miles to Caernarfon. Two members of the crew are put ashore and set off on the 24-mile round trip to the top of Snowdon, Wales' highest mountain. There follows a 92-mile voyage to Ravenglass and the ascent of Scafell Pike, England's loftiest peak, and a 32-mile hike. Fort William, 235 nautical miles away, is the next port of call from where Ben Nevis must be scaled. The 17-mile slog involves a climb of over 4,000ft. The first crew back from this climb wins the race.

INTO THE DEPTHS

The traditional markings on a leadline

Two fathoms	Two strips of leather
Three fathoms	Three strips of leather
Five fathoms	A piece of white rag
Seven fathoms	A piece of red bunting
10 fathoms	A piece of leather with a hole in it
13 fathoms	A piece of blue serge
15 fathoms	Another piece of white rag
17 fathoms	Another piece of red bunting
20 fathoms	Two knots

Leadlines should be wetted and stretched prior to marking.
One fathom equals six feet, or 1.8288 metres.

SUBMARINE SAFETY

There have been several incidents when fishing vessels and even yachts have disappeared at sea and submarines have been thought to be responsible. If you are worried about submarine accidents you should run your engine or generator, even when under sail, and keep your echo sounder switched on. You should also show deck-level navigation lights at night on the pulpit and stern. It is common sense to stay clear of charted submarine exercise areas and away from any vessel flying code flags 'NE2' meaning that submarines are in the vicinity. Subfacts – warnings of planned or known submarine activity – are broadcast by local coastguard stations.

ALL AT SEA

'And I say this would have never happened if we'd bought a caravan instead of this bloody boat.'

It's commonly believed (by those who stay ashore) that a camaraderie exists among those who go to sea – but nothing could be further from the truth. The sad fact is that there are as many divisions, rivalries and prejudices at sea as there are on land. It's a minefield for anyone new to boating, but there are some basic rules.

1 Anyone who is paid to go to sea has little time or respect for those who do so for pleasure. A fisherman is only pleased to see a yacht if it has lost its mast and is about to be washed onto the rocks, so he can tow it to safety and claim thousands of pounds of salvage.

2 The crew of supertankers and container ships have even less regard for leisure sailors. Yachtsmen may think that power gives way to sail, but it takes four miles to slow down a supertanker and they work to strict timetables. They will not stop for some fool with a sail – especially since the bridge is often unmanned and the radar set to only pick up another ship that could do it damage – not an eminently crunchable yacht.

3 The yachtsman has his own enemies; motorboats, or 'stinkpots' as he calls them, are considered vulgar by the majority of yachtsmen. They shatter the peace, kick up a huge wake and are often owned by men with tattoos. The fact that these vulgar fellows' boats cost 10 times as much as most yachts has nothing to do with this sailing snobbery. Perish the thought!

4 Of course motorboaters don't take this lying down. Instead they invite each other over for a drink and chuckle about the stupidity of yachtsmen – or 'raggies', as they call them. Yachts are tippy, uncomfortable, dangerous and spend half the time motoring anyway. 'So I drive a stinkpot, do I?' laughs the motorboater. 'At least I'm not a WAFI*!' And he and his friends fall about.

*Wind Assisted F*****g Idiot

FIND THE COMFY SPOT

There is, in every cockpit, a perfect place to sit. This will vary from boat to boat and will also vary according to the angle at which she is sailing. Most cockpits are comfortable in harbour, but when the yacht starts to heel, you suddenly find that you've got a winch in your back or that the mainsail traveller is threatening to slice off your fingers, or worse. You need somewhere to settle, with good support, out of the worst of the weather and where you won't get in the way. The three favourite spots are:

1   Huddled with your back to the cabin bulkhead, looking astern and out of the wind.

2   Right at the stern, in one corner or the other. You should be safe from spray here and can nestle against the pushpit – considerably more comfortable than the wires of the guardrails further forward.

3   The companionway. Everyone seems to be drawn to the stairs at a party and it is the same on yachts. Standing on the steps down to the cabin allows you to see what is going on, and feel part of it all, without putting your boots on. However, just as at a party, such stair dwellers get in the way of those trying to get past and you'll eventually be moved on – although it won't be long before someone takes your place.

SEA SAYINGS

Wipe the slate clean
A slate tablet was kept near the helm on which the watch keeper would record the speeds, distances, headings and tacks during the watch. If the slate was wiped clean at the start of a new watch all previous incidents could be forgotten.

NAVAL TOASTS

Monday	Our ships at sea
Tuesday	Our men
Wednesday	Ourselves
Thursday	A bloody war or a sickly season
Friday	A willing foe and sea room
Saturday	Sweethearts and wives (may they never meet)
Sunday	Absent friends

Thursday's toast harks back to the days when promotion came only on the death of a superior officer. Friday's toast stems from the fact that success in battles meant a share of the bounty for the commanding officers.

HERE BE MONSTERS

Tales of strange sea creatures that attack boats and drag sailors to their deaths have been around for as long as men have gone to sea. Ancient charts illustrate strange sea monsters and giant fish – usually at the extremities of the charted areas. Few people believe in sea monsters these days, yet still many mysteries lie beneath the sea.

Whales and large sharks probably gave rise to the first tales of sea monsters, and both have been known to attack ships, but it's the giant squid that keeps the sea monster myth alive.

Architeutis dux is the largest of all invertebrates, reaching some 60ft in length. Recent sightings describe giant squid more than 130ft long and round-the-world yachtsmen have reported 30ft squid attaching themselves to their boats, but marine biologists have yet to observe a giant squid alive.

Exploration of the deepest, darkest depths is only just beginning, with remote submarines allowing cameras to discover new creatures that exist far beyond man's realm. Perhaps there be monsters after all.

THE QUARTERMASTER'S STORES

Here is the traditional sailor's ditty in full – ideal for long
boat journeys:

> *There were rats, rats, big as blooming cats,*
> *In the stores, in the stores.*
> *There were rats, rats, big as blooming cats,*
> *In the quartermaster's stores.*
> *My eyes are dim, I cannot see,*
> *I have not got my specs with me,*
> *I have not got my specs with me.*

Depending on the length of your journey, you might need
the rest of the verses...

> Mice ... *running through the rice*
> Snakes ... *as big as garden rakes*
> Beans ... *as big as submarines*
> Gravy ... *enough to float the navy*
> Cakes ... *that give us tummy aches*
> Eggs ... *with scaly chicken legs*
> Butter ... *running in the gutter*
> Lard ... *they sell it by the yard*
> Bread ... *with great big lumps like lead*
> Cheese ... *that makes you want to sneeze*
> Soot ... *they grow it by the foot*
> Goats ... *eating all the oats*
> Bees ... *with little knobby knees*
> Owls ... *shredding paper towels*
> Apes ... *eating all the grapes*
> Turtles ... *wearing rubber girdles*
> Bear ... *with curlers in its hair*
> Buffaloes ... *with hair between their toes*
> Foxes ... *stuffed in little boxes*
> Coke ... *enough to make you choke*
> Pepsi ... *that gives you apoplexy*
> Flies ... *swarming round the pies*
> Fishes ... *sitting in the dishes*
> Moths ... *eating through the cloth*
> Scouts ... *eating brussels sprouts*

ALL AT SEA

Jonah agreed to put the armour on only after the crew promised that it would help him float.

NAUTICAL PUZZLES

Rearrange this observation to discover the first rule of sinking:
Trim candid Helen frowns
Answer on page 145

SAILING TERMS THAT
CONFUSE LANDLUBBERS
Tack

A shop that is full of tack will contain a variety of novelty cruet sets, posters of cats in amusing poses and plastic fish that sing to you each time you walk past. A stable that is full of tack will have saddles, crops, stirrups and bridles hanging from every wall. You can even use a tack to hold down a carpet. But ignore all that. When sailing, to tack means to change course by passing the bow of the boat through the wind. Such a manoeuvre is consequently known as a tack. Simple – except that you have to remember that tack also refers to the lower forward corner of a sail.

DO YOU WANT ICE WITH THAT?

For home waters sailors, ice is just an innocent ingredient in the aprés sail G&T, but for those voyaging to the high latitudes, it poses a grave threat. Taking the temperature of the air of the water is not a reliable way to detect the proximity of an iceberg, nor is listening for an echo from a whistle or siren. More reliable indications that an iceberg is nearby include coming across an area of calm water in open sea, suggesting that an iceberg is to windward. A sound like gunfire may be the noise of part of an iceberg breaking off to create a growler. The sound of waves breaking on the shore when there is no nearby land is another chilling indication that an iceberg is nearby.

NAUTICAL PUZZLES

Rearrange this sentence to discover where this action takes place:
He eases vents
Answer on page 145

One of the greatest acts of seamanship ever undertaken in the last 100 years was that of Sir Ernest Shackleton on board a small open boat called the *James Caird*. Shackleton had been bound for Antarctica on the ship *Endurance* when she was caught in the ice and crushed. He and his crew had to leave her, take the ship's small lifeboats and seek dry land on 9 April 1916. This they did, but were little better off as they were then marooned on Elephant Island, 800 miles south of Cape Horn, with little food and no chance of rescue. Shackleton ordered for the *James Caird*, a 23ft whaler, to be modified with a deck and extra ballast.

On 24 April he set sail with five companions bound for South Georgia, 500 miles away. It was winter in the Antarctic and conditions were appalling for the men, who did not have the benefit of modern clothing or navigation equipment. Shackleton and his crew survived constant storms, giant waves and icebergs and made landfall on South Georgia after 14 days at sea. However they were far from saved as they had landed on the uninhabited side of the island and faced a near-impossible crossing of the island's frozen and mountainous interior. However, against all odds they made it.

The next morning Shackleton left on a whaler to rescue the men he had left on Elephant Island. However pack ice forced the ship back on that and two subsequent rescue attempts. It was fourth time lucky on 30 August 1916, when Shackleton's ship was sighted. Within hours the 23 men were safely returning to a world that had heard no news from them since October 1914; they had survived on Elephant Island for 105 days. Their extraordinary experiences would make them famous, and the leadership and seamanship of Shackleton would make him a hero.

THE REALITY OF SAILING

Toast

It may seem a very petty moan but the fact that you can't get a good piece of toast at sea is something that can weigh heavily on a yachtsman's mind during a long cruise or ocean passage. Some yachts have a socket into which a toaster can be plugged, but these normally work only when one is in harbour and connected into power from the shore. Ovens can be bought that include grills, but these can be expensive. The average sailor is therefore left with making toast on his gas hob. As much thought and ingenuity has been put into how to do this successfully as has been devoted to the design of any other piece of yachting equipment. There are numerous contraptions that seek to diffuse the heat of the flame and turn bread from soft and white to crisp and golden brown, but none of them succeed. The result is almost always a burnt exterior while the inside of the bread is totally uncooked. There is, in addition, an inevitable taste of gas to the 'toast'. Some sailors throw their toasters overboard and buy crispbread instead. Others waft their slice of bread over the flame, like some Victorian pantry maid with a toasting fork. Using a dry non-stick saucepan is also alleged to work though is yet to catch on.

The simple truth is that if you want a perfect piece of toast you will have to stay at home.

WHERE YACHTSMEN SHOULD LIVE

Hull
Keele
Rock
Sale
Winchester

I THINK I'LL BUILD MY BOAT WITH...

Wood

Wood certainly has its appeal as a boatbuilding material. Natural beauty comes high on most people's lists – there is something very special about wood that continues to live and breathe long after it has been felled. It may be roughly hewn and weather-beaten, or it might be immaculately varnished, but wood speaks to a sailor's soul as no other material can. The fact that wood floats, unlike most other materials used to build boats, probably makes it attractive at some subconscious level.

That's the romance; in practice it can be a different matter. Wood demands care and attention like no other material. It will look after you only if you look after it. That means plenty of painting and varnishing, tracking down leaks and tackling rot and worm. The wooden boats that are being built today tend to be very beautiful and very expensive.

NOT THAT TOUR DE FRANCE

The French love their cycling and the Tour de France is the greatest cycling race in the world. They also love their sailing, a fact reflected by the interest the nation has in the Tour de France *à la Voile*.

The racing takes place among a fleet of identical Mumm 30 yachts, designed by Bruce Farr. The boats are fast and exciting yet relatively uncomplicated and economical, making them attractive to sponsors. The events are held at the same time as the cycle race and involve a series of races along the English Channel, the Atlantic Coast and the Mediterranean. There are inshore thrashes as well as coastal hops, allowing skippers and crews to show off their skills in a wide variety of conditions. Professional teams race for line honours in each event but the large fleet also includes a number of amateur and student crews.

GLAD TIDINGS

The oceans are subject to the gravitational pull of the moon and sun. These forces, coupled with the rotation of the Earth, give rise to the tides that cause the water level to rise and fall around our coasts. The coming and going of this water results in tidal streams and these can dramatically help or hinder a sailor trying to get from A to B. The direction and rates of tide are recorded in Tidal Atlases, allowing a sailor to see whether the movement of the water will be with or against him. If it's with, he may be in port an hour or two sooner, if against, he may not get there at all. Sailing against a foul tide (one that is running in the opposite direction to that in which you want to go) is like walking up the down escalator: plenty of movement but no progress.

Tides are often accelerated as they are pushed around headlands or between land-masses. Tides of around two knots are common around Britain's coast, although flows of 16 knots have been recorded off the coast of Scotland.

KEEPING YOUR WOOD DRY

If a wooden boat absorbs water it will eventually rot. Various methods are used to prevent moisture absorption, though some are more effective than others.

Coating	Efficiency after 28 days (%)
Enamel	58
Oil paint	50
Lead paint	45
Varnish	20
Pink primer	14
Wax polish	3
Boiled oil and turps	>2
Raw linseed oil	>2

WATERSPOUTS

Waterspouts are perhaps the most spectacular meteorological phenomenon that can be witnessed at sea. They are essentially mini tornados and can occur anywhere that the water is noticeably warmer than the air and there are thunderclouds forming.

Cold air is warmed by the warmer water and starts to rise, and this process is exaggerated by the thundercloud above that sucks up the warm moist air. In these unstable conditions a bulge of cloud can emerge from the bottom of the thundercloud with powerful downdrafts of wind. These downdrafts are matched by the swirling of air upwards. These two actions result in a swirling effect and the bulge becomes a rotating trunk. The trunk sucks up warm air, which is full of energy, making it larger and more powerful. When the trunk reaches the water, more energy is added to the equation, with warm water being sucked upwards, intensifying the process even more. Winds inside a waterspout can reach 150 knots and while it is extremely rare for a yacht to be struck by one, the effects are normally devastating. If you see a waterspout forming while afloat, sail at right angles to the direction in which the clouds are travelling.

TYPES OF ROPE

Type of rope	Key properties
Polypropylene	Cheap, light, floats
Nylon	Strong and stretchy
Polyester	Strong, low stretch
High Modulus Polyethylene	Strong, light low stretch
Vectran	Very strong, very low stretch
PBO	Exceptionally strong, very low stretch, very expensive

A NAUTICAL LIMERICK

There was a young sailor named Bates
Who danced the fandango on skates.
He fell on his cutlass
Which rendered him nutless
And practically useless on dates.

BEST SCILLY BEACHES

The Isles of Scilly are a dream destination for many yachtsmen. Lying in the warming Gulf Stream current they boast a semi-tropical climate and in settled weather could easily be mistaken for a corner of the Caribbean. There are many anchorages, though none offers protection from all directions, making a trip to the Scillies something of a gamble. If you do sail there you will be able to explore the countless stunning beaches that fringe the islands. According to the islanders, the top 10 beaches are:

1. Great Bay on St Martin's
2. Pentle Bay on Tresco
3. Rushy Bay on Bryher
4. Pelistry Bay on St Mary's
5. The Bar on St Agnes
6. Bar Point on St Mary's
7. Lawrence's Beach on St Martin's
8. Landing Beach on Samson
9. Appletree Bay on Tresco
10. Great Porth on Bryher

NAUTICAL PUZZLES

Whose company is preferable during severe weather:
Taylor's or Graham's?
Answer on page 145

WALLS OF WATER

Waves pose a far greater threat to the safety of sailors than does the wind. A well-found (well-built, solid) vessel with enough sea room can ride out high winds as long as the seas do not become too rough. But freak waves can strike ships almost out of the blue.

Rogue waves emerge from relatively calm seas with no storms for hundreds of miles. Trains of swells travelling in the same direction but at different speeds will pass through one another; when their crests, troughs and lengths happen to coincide they reinforce each other, combining energies to form unusually large waves that tower for a few minutes then subside. Such giants can suddenly reach several times the height of the waves around them, forming mid-ocean breakers that are probably responsible for at least some mysterious disappearances of ships.

REASONS TO GO TO NEWLYN

Few yachtsmen venture beyond the granite mass of Cornwall's Lizard peninsula to the ports of Penzance and Newlyn. The wreck-strewn coastland puts many sailors off, although those who do go the extra mile are rewarded. Not only does Newlyn boast one of the country's busiest fish markets, it also hosts a unique tidal observatory.

The observatory is located at the end of the harbour's south pier and was established to determine the mean sea level that is used to calculate sea-level measurements across the UK. The mean sea level by which all others are measured was determined between 1915 and 1921 when the height of the water was noted every 15 minutes, 24 hours a day, every day of the year. From these observations the mean sea level was established and is marked by a brass bolt set into the ground.

HAVE A WHALE OF A TIME

Yachtsmen have a special relationship with animals that live in the sea. There are many stories of single-handed yachtsmen who refuse to catch fish because they feel some strange bond with these creatures for whom the sea is also their world. Some fish will swim for thousands of miles in the shadow cast by a yacht's hull and there are sailors who develop a real fondness for these scaly companions. Other yachtsmen save their affections for fellow mammals with whom they share the sea.

Porpoises, dolphins and whales are naturally drawn to yachts, whether out of curiosity, playfulness or to establish that there is no risk from these strange intruders into their world. Dolphins are a particular delight and their playfulness is legendary. It is not uncommon for sailors to come across pods containing too many dolphins to count and a display of aquatic acrobatics is almost guaranteed. Then, as quickly as the dolphins come, they go again, leaving you in silent awe of their grace and speed.

Whales are even more impressive, though seen less often. They are also feared by many sailors, and with good reason. Hitting a whale can be catastrophic for a small boat. The whale will probably escape with a headache, but the yacht is more likely to spring a leak that could sink it. Mid-ocean collisions are frighteningly common but happen so quickly that it is often impossible to determine what has been struck.

Not that all whale encounters are accidental. Tales are told of whales attacking yachts and it's a worrying time for any skipper when he knows he is sailing through a pod of whales. These mighty mammals will often swim very close to boats before submerging. The wait is agonising – will the creature rise up beneath the keel and up-end the yacht, or leave it to sail on? Attacks are rare, though in the summer of 2003 a yacht chartered by an English family was attacked by a whale while sailing among the Whitsunday Islands, off Australia. The whale rose up from the water and crashed down on the yacht, smashing its rigging and knocking its mast down. It is thought that the yacht had sailed between a mother whale and her calf and she reacted as any mother would.

It is always a treat to sail with dolphins and whales and their unpredictability is just one of the things that makes these encounters so thrilling.

WHO'S BEEN TELLING TALES?

Non-sailors watch with awe as the yachtsman pulls in one rope, lets out another, sucks his teeth, glances aloft and then declares the sails are properly set. It may seem like dark magic, but the basic techniques of sail trim are surprisingly easy as long as the sails are fitted with telltales. These strands of wool or sailcloth are attached to specific parts of the mainsail and genoa (the large triangular front sail) and indicate how the wind is flowing over them. If they fly horizontally with little fluttering you know that you are doing something right – if not then you'll need to pull in or let out a sheet, change the boat's angle to the wind, or adjust one of the other lines that controls the sail's shape.

Sailing by the genoa telltales is perhaps easiest of all. Take the helm in one hand and sit on the leeward side of the boat. Fix the genoa telltales with a beady eye and watch what they are doing. If the telltales on the windward side of the sail start to lift, then steer away from the wind; if the ones on the other side lift, then steer towards the wind. If both sides are flying straight and true then do nothing. Simple!

Charts change. This may be because a buoy has been placed over a new hazard, or because a sand bank has appeared where once there was deep water. Cartographers can make mistakes too – an alarming but unavoidable fact.

To ensure he is carrying the most accurate chart, a sailor must check to see if any of his charts have been updated. All hydrographic offices issue regular corrections, in the form of Notices to Mariners, for their paper and electronic charts. Private paper chartmakers do the same. The notices tell you what to cross out, add or move. If there are complicated changes to a small area then a 'patch' will be issued. This is a piece of the chart that can be cut out and stuck over the area of chart to be amended.

Until five or six years ago, Notices to Mariners were issued in paper form on a weekly basis, with monthly and annual summaries. There was then an intermediate period in which most hydrographic offices also made them available on the internet. Over the past year some hydrographic offices (including the British Admiralty) have been phasing out the paper version. Access to the internet is now essential to keep charts updated and shows how technology has become part of all sailors' lives, whether they like it or not.

SEA SAYINGS

I don't like the cut of his jib

In days gone by, warships often had foresails (or jibs) shaped so that they could sail close to the wind and thus catch vessels to windward of them. Upon sighting these easily recognised foresails on a distant ship, a captain might declare that he did not like the cut of the other fellow's jib and attempt to flee.

OYSTER DREDGERS

Set sail on the River Fal on a chill autumn day and you will not be alone. The yachtsmen who sail for pleasure will probably be sitting snug in their marinas, leaving the waters of the Fal to the men who sail for a living. But these are not professional racers with six-figure salaries: they are Cornishmen dredging for oysters.

Local regulations prohibit the use of power-driven vessels with which to dredge for oysters and so the fishermen do it the old-fashioned way. With a scrap of sail hoisted, they make their way to windward, their nets scouring the riverbed for the oysters that will fetch a high price in the markets of London and beyond. Dredging by sail in a traditional working boat is less efficient than using a modern boat with an engine and powered winches, and so the oyster stocks are not depleted, meaning the industry can continue from one year to the next. It's a piece of practical ecological legislation that means hard work for the men who sail the boats, but creates a future for the industry and is a wonderful sight for anyone who sees these skilled sailors at work.

WATCH UP, DOC?

Time	Name	Abbreviated name
0001-0400	Middle Watch	Middle (Hey Diddle Diddle)
0400-0800	Morning Watch	The Morning
0800-1200	Forenoon Watch	The Forenoon
1200-1600	Afternoon Watch	The Afternoon
1600-1800	First Dog Watch	First Dog
1800-2000	Last Dog	Last Dog
2000-0001	First Watch	The First (Geoff Hurst)
All Night in Bed	'All Night in'	(Rin Tin Tin)

THE PLIGHT OF THE ALBATROSS

The albatross occupies a special place in the heart of anyone who has spent time on the world's oceans. Sometimes these amazing birds will be your only companion for days, your only contact with the world beyond your vessel's hull.

And amazing they are. With its 12ft wingspan, an albatross can fly up to 1,615 miles in 24 hours, diving into waves to collect food ploughed up by the keels of ships. But now the albatross is falling victim to deep-sea fishing boats trailing 80-mile long lines covered with thousands upon thousands of hooks. Each hook is baited with squid to persuade valuable fish to bite and secure their fate as Japanese sushi. But more than 100,000 albatrosses fall victim to these lures a year. These fishing fleets operate beyond the law and have no concerns other than the price their catch will fetch. The fact that the albatross may join the dodo is of no interest to them, though international pressure may help stop deaths. To learn more, visit www.panda.org.

OLYMPIC SAILING BOATS AND CLASSES

Equipment	Event
Europe	Women's Single-handed Dinghy
Finn	Men's Single-handed Dinghy
470 Men	Men's Double-handed Dinghy
470 Women	Women's Double-handed Dinghy
49er	Open Double-handed High Performance Dinghy
Laser	Open Single-handed Dinghy
Mistral Men	Men's Windsurfer
Mistral Women	Women's Windsurfer
Star	Men's Double-handed Keelboat
Tornado	Open Double-handed Multihull
Yngling	Women's Triple-handed Keelboat

FIRE!

Fire and boats do not mix. There are, of course, large amounts of water available to put out the fire, but by the time you've thrown a bucket over the side, hauled it on board and thrown it on to the inferno, the flames may have got the upper hand. Fire was a constant hazard on naval sailing ships and in 1568 an order was given to the entire British fleet regarding measures that should be put in place so that fires could be quickly extinguished.

The captain was to order that two large casks be cut in half and chained securely. 'The soldiers and mariners to piss in them that they may always be full of urine to quench fire work with, and two or three pieces of old sail ready to wet the piss; and always cast it on the fire work as need shall require.' Effective though it was, modern mariners now use fire extinguishers instead.

SEASICKNESS

The dreaded *mal de mer* can strike even the hardiest yachtsman. Many of the great voyagers spent the first few days at sea with their head over the side, feeding the fish. Tracy Edwards, famed skipper of *Maiden*, the all-girl round the world yacht, is reputed to do little but feed the fish for 36 hours before she finds her sea legs.

Cures for seasickness are legion and while some may work for some sailors some of the time, none work for all sailors all of the time. Ginger biscuits are meant to help, as is scanning the horizon or taking a turn at the helm. Drugs help some but send others to sleep. One patch that is placed behind the ear has been known to cause hallucinations – not what you need in the middle of a night watch.

There is one remedy that always works and the unafflicted take great joy in telling their stricken shipmate about it. The magic cure? To sit under a tree.

SEA SAYINGS

Taken aback/take the wind out of your sails

A sudden shift of wind or slip in the helmsman's concentration can lead to the wind blowing on the wrong side of a warship's sails, putting massive pressure on rigging and masts and making the ship unsteady. This unwelcome situation was always unexpected and could take the wind out of your sails, quite literally.

WHERE AM I?

The Global Positioning System (GPS) has changed the face of navigation forever. Just a few decades ago the idea of a small box no bigger than a mobile phone being able to provide your precise latitude and longitude seemed the stuff of science fiction. Today it is almost taken for granted.

GPS consists of 24 satellites circling the earth in six orbital planes at 55 degrees to the Equator. Three extra satellites are up there as active spares, waiting to take over if another satellite fails. The satellites beam down information, giving their own position at a given time. The delay between the information being transmitted and received on the ground is used to calculate the distance between the satellite and the receiver. With this information from three satellites, three intersecting range circles can be formed. The receiver is located where the circles cross.

The accuracy of GPS was artificially reduced until 2000 to prevent countries outside the West using it for military purposes. The Standard Positioning Service now available to yachtsmen is accurate to within about 20 metres, and current technological advances should improve accuracy to within 2 metres in the very near future.

I NAME THIS SHIP

The US Navy has an unofficial tradition of naming certain types of ship after certain things…

Type of Craft	Named After
Aircraft carriers	battles, famous Americans
Ammunition ships	volcanoes, fire/explosion terms
Amphibious command ships	mountains, mountain ranges
Battleships	US states
Cargo ships	heavenly bodies, US counties
Cruisers	US cities
Destroyer tenders	US locations and areas
Destroyers	late Navy and Marine Corps heroes
Hospital ships	assistance-related mission terms
Minesweepers	danger-related terms
Nuclear submarines	famous Americans
Oilers	rivers, shipbuilders
Store ships	heavenly bodies
Submarine rescue vessels	birds
Older submarines	fish and sea creatures
Tugboats	Native American tribes and terms

A TYPICAL YEAR IN THE RNLI

Crew member hours at sea: 53,732

Services to people: 2,215 *(27.3% of total services)*

Services to merchant/fishing vessels: 948 *(11.7% of total services)*

Services carried out in darkness: 2,987 (36.8% of total services)

Services to pleasure craft: 4,209 *(51.9% of total services)*

Services carried out in winds of Force Seven plus: 157 *(1.9% of total services)*

HOW TO FIRE A CANNON

Should you ever find yourself required to fire a cannon,
these orders – as issued by a captain in Nelson's navy – to
fire and reload a loaded stowed cannon might come in
handy:

Silence!
Cast loose your gun!
Level your gun!
Take out your tampion!
Prime!
Run out your gun!
Fire!
Worm and sponge!
Load with cartridge!
Load with shot and wad your shot!
Ram home shot and wad!
Put in your tampion!
House your gun!
Secure your gun!

EARTHQUAKE!

You might think that an earthquake is the one hazard you
wouldn't face at sea – but you'd be wrong. Severe quakes
can cause tidal waves or shift the seabed so dramatically
that you can be afloat one minute and aground the next.
The Hydrographic Department of the Ministry of Defence
has records of the damage caused by an earthquake off the
coast of Portugal in 1969. The crew on one ship 100 miles
away felt violent vibrations for about a minute. Another
vessel the same distance away experienced a severe vertical
shock. Meanwhile a motor tanker just 15 miles from the
epicentre was lifted upwards and slammed down with such
heavy vibrations that she was subsequently condemned as
a total loss.

FLASH – AAH!

You can see many spectacular natural phenomena at sea. Waterspouts and whirlpools are impressive but the rarest and most magical sight of all is the green flash at sunset.

If conditions are just right, a bright flash appears along the horizon just as the sun is sinking beyond view. Those who have witnessed it say that it is incomparable.

The green flash happens so rarely that it has taken on a mythological status among seafarers, but there is a perfectly good explanation for the marine pyrotechnics.

The flash is caused by refractive separation of the sun's rays into its spectral components. The curvature of the Earth means that as the sun sets it shines through the sea with the water acting as a filter – when refractive conditions are suitable, red, orange and yellow waves of sunlight are not refracted sufficiently to reach the eye, whereas green waves are. The visual result is a green flash in the surrounding sky.

HELICOPTER AHOY

On large vessels the following equipment should be to hand if a helicopter is about to land, to drop off or pick up people or goods:

Portable fire extinguisher
Large axe
Crowbar
Wire cutters
Static discharge/earthing pole
Red emergency signal/torch
Marshalling batons (at night)
First aid equipment

This equipment is not necessary on a yacht, but you must follow the helicopter pilot's instructions precisely and never attach any lines from the helicopter to the boat.

PERILS OF THE SEA

'A spot of trouble at the windward mark meant that sailing would not reappear as an Olympic sport for many years.

I THINK I'LL BUILD MY BOAT FROM...

Aluminium

Most people compare aluminium to steel, the other raw material of choice if building a metal boat. It's certainly more expensive – 10 times or more – and is only about 65% as strong. So why use it? The reason is weight. It's only one third as heavy and that means an aluminium boat will be much faster than her steel sister.

It may not be pretty but aluminium can be left bare, unlike most other materials, and requires the minimum of maintenance. It won't rust but is highly vulnerable to electrolysis and corrosion when in contact with other metals. Aluminium is stronger than other 'traditional' materials, meaning that you may be able to escape from a severe grounding that would have sunk a wooden or GRP boat.

SOUNDS AT SEA

Sound signals used when vessels are in sight
of one another

One short blast *I am altering my course to starboard*

Two short blasts *I am altering my course to port*

Three short blasts *My engines are going astern*

Five short blasts *I am unsure of your intentions*

Four short blasts, one short blast *I intend to turn completely around to starboard*

Four short blasts, two short blasts *I intend to turn completely around to port*

Two long blasts, one short blast *I wish to overtake you on your starboard side*

Two long blasts, two short blasts *I wish to overtake you on your port side*

One long blast, one short blast, one long blast, one short blast *You may overtake me on the side indicated*

SAILING TERMS THAT
CONFUSE LANDLUBBERS

Spar

To some this is a convenient local store selling overpriced toilet paper, to others it is a boxing workout, and to the hard of spelling it is a health resort. However, at sea a spar is none of these. For 'spar', read 'big stick', as spars are the masts, booms and other big sticks from which the sails are hoisted and held aloft.

Originally all spars were the trunks and branches of trees, but hollow metal masts were found to be lighter and now high-tech carbon spars are de rigueur on extreme racing yachts. This may help a yacht sail faster, but broken masts can no longer be replaced by stolen telegraph poles, as they could in the good old days.

Kite-surfing is the most extreme form of sailing and one of the fastest-growing sports in the world. On almost any long, sandy beach you are likely to see someone with a wet suit, a small surfboard and a large kite. The kite-surfer wears a harness to which the kite is attached and has two lines to control the kite: pull left to go left, right to go right. It may sound simple, but in practice it is another matter.

Keeping the expanse of canvas in the air above you while you wade into the surf and attempt to attach your board is very difficult – and you haven't even started the surfing bit yet. A quick pull on one of the strings, and you are away, skimming over the water with one eye on the sea and the other on the kite – as soon as it stops moving you start to sink. To keep the kite up, the surfer must tug his strings so that it stays in the 'power zone' – go too far to one side or the other and it will stop pulling and eventually collapse.

If the kite ends up in the drink all is not lost. One edge is inflatable and is pumped up before launching. If the kite crashes, it will remain afloat and a couple of tugs of the line should have it soaring into the air again.

The fact that the kites pull up as well as along allows skilled kite-surfers to perform incredible stunts, literally hanging in the air as they twist and turn. A professional circuit is now well-established and a range of disciplines allow all aspects of this thrilling sport to be showcased. There are also open water races with fleets of kite-surfers flitting across the water beneath the colourful canopies of their kites.

But not all sailors are thrilled by the popularity of kite-surfing. The sport attracts thrill seekers who may have little idea of nautical rules. Kite-surfers can easily exceed 20 knots as they skim across the water and some yachtsmen see them as hazard.

THE ROUND THE ISLAND RACE

Every summer the waters of the Solent are virtually obscured for one day by the hundreds of yachts that compete in a race around the Isle of Wight. First sailed in 1931, the competitors in the Round the Island Race still compete for the Gold Roman Bowl, the legendary trophy presented by the race's founder Cyril Windeler. Little did he realise what he was starting.

Today, there are often more than 1,500 yachts, from maxi-yachts to the smallest offshore categories, and from speedy multihulls to sedate old-timers. With Admirals Cuppers competing alongside families having fun, the race is a multitude of races within a race. The start line is nautical chaos as the weekend cruisers get in the way of the hardcore racers and nimble sports boats flying past. Once past the rocks and wrecks of the Needles, things calm down a little, though if the tide is not kind and the wind is not strong, the stragglers may find themselves still at sea while the fastest crews are snug in the beer tent.

HOW TO ABANDON SHIP

A few points to remember if you need to take to your life raft:

Abandon ship only as a last resort.
If you have time, take extra food, water and
distress equipment.
Attach the raft's painter to the yacht before launching it.
Put the fittest and strongest person on board first
to help others in.
Cut yourself free of the yacht only if there is a risk
of its sinking – it is a bigger target for rescuers to find.
Take seasickness tablets – being sick will weaken you.
Do not drink seawater or urine.

ANCIENT MARINERS

Gerald had started to act differently since being made commodore of the yacht club.

WHAT'S THE BOTTOM LIKE?

Types of seabed as found on United Kingdom Hydrographic Office charts:

Algae • Basalt • Boulders • Cinders • Clay • Cobbles
Coral • Diatoms • Foram inifera • Glauconite • Gravel
Ground • Kelp • Lava • Madrepore • Manganese
Marl • Mussels • Mud • Ooze • Oysters • Pebbles
Polyzoa • Pteropods • Pumice • Quartz • Radiolaria
Rock • Sandwaves • Sand • Scoriae • Shells • Shingle
Silt • Spring in seabed • Sponge • Stones • Tufa • Weed

THE REALITY OF SAILING

Anchoring

There is a feeling among the sailing community that too many yachtsmen go from marina to marina, never stopping for the night at one of the countless anchorages around Britain's coast. Look closer and it becomes clear why this is so. On arrival at an anchorage there are bound to be a few yachts there before you. Each will have a skipper who will be keeping a keen eye on your movements in case you do anything to endanger his vessel. He'll shout the second that you start to drop the hook in the wrong place, but is unlikely to stand on the fore deck and cheerfully point out where his anchor is actually lying so that you can make a properly informed decision about where to drop your own. In the absence of such knowledge you'll just have to guess and hope all will be well.

If the anchor holds then it'll be time to put the kettle on and wait for the next yacht to turn up so that you can watch them go through the same process. If you're not sure of your holding then you must hoist the hook and start all over again.

Perhaps you want to go ashore? Out with the dinghy and the pump and the oars and maybe the outboard too. But what if the wind shifts or someone fouls your anchor and sets you adrift? Best to play safe and stay put. Supper can be eaten in the cockpit, until the rain starts and you have to go below. But careful with the lights – you don't want to run the battery flat. And so to bed and blissful sleep – but what was that noise? Has the wind started to freshen already? Are you swinging? Has your transit shifted. No? Fine, back to half-sleep until the next grumble of anchor-chain over rock. Dawn comes and you set sail for the nearest marina and a bit of relaxation and not to mention a good night's sleep.

133

BEAUFORT WIND SCALE

Francis Beaufort was born in 1774 in County Meath, Ireland and began his nautical career aged 13 as a cabin boy in the Navy. He served in the Navy for 68 years, rising to the rank of Rear Admiral. He invented his famous wind scale in 1806 and it was adopted by the Royal Navy in 1838. It has changed little since.

Force	Wind (knots)	Description	Effects on the water	Effects on land
0	< 1	Calm	Sea surface smooth and mirror-like	Calm, smoke rises vertically
1	1-3	Light Air	Scaly ripples, no foam crests	Smoke drift indicates wind direction, still wind vanes
2	4-6	Light Breeze	Small wavelets, crests glassy, no breaking	Wind felt on face, leaves rustle, vanes begin to move
3	7-10	Gentle Breeze	Large wavelets, crests begin to break, scattered whitecaps	Leaves and small twigs constantly moving, light flags extended
4	11-16	Moderate Breeze	Small waves, 1-4ft, becoming longer, numerous whitecaps	Dust, leaves, and loose paper lifted, small tree branches move
5	17-21	Fresh Breeze	Moderate waves, 4-8ft, taking longer form, many whitecaps, some spray	Small trees in leaf begin to sway
6	22-27	Strong Breeze	Larger waves, 8-13ft, whitecaps common, more spray	Larger tree branches moving, whistling in wires

Force	Wind (knots)	Description	Effects on the water	Effects on land
7	28-33	Near Gale	Sea heaps up, waves 13-20ft, white foam streaks off breakers	Whole trees moving, resistance felt walking against wind
8	34-40	Gale	Moderately high (13-20ft) waves of greater length, edges of crests begin to break into spindrift, foam blown in streaks	Whole trees in motion, resistance felt walking against wind
9	41-47	Strong Gale	High waves (20ft), sea begins to roll, dense streaks of foam, spray may reduce visibility	Slight structural damage occurs, slate blows off roofs
10	48-55	Storm	Very high waves (20-30ft) with overhanging crests, sea white with densely blown foam, heavy rolling, lowered visibility	Seldom experienced on land, trees broken or uprooted, 'considerable structural damage'
11	56-63	Violent Storm	Exceptionally high (30-45ft) waves, foam patches cover sea, visibility more reduced	
12	64+	Hurricane	Air filled with foam, waves over 45ft, sea completely white with driving spray, visibility greatly reduced	[no land indication as trees and buildings have already been flattened]

QUOTES ON BOATS

Loose lips sink ships.
World War II poster slogan

HOW TO GET KNOTTED

The reef knot

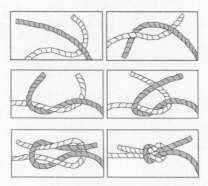

Take the left working end and cross it over and under the right working end.

Now tuck the new right working end over and under the new working end on the left. Pull both the working ends to tighten.

Alternatively: left over right, under and through; right over left, under and through.

SEA SAYINGS

No room to swing a cat

Not the literal meaning that many people imagine. On naval ships the entire ship's company was required to witness flogging at close hand. The crew would crowd around, meaning that the Bosun's Mate often barely had enough room to swing his cat o' nine tails whip.

NELSON'S PRAYER

On the morning of 21 October 1805, with the combined fleets of France and Spain then in sight, Nelson wrote this prayer in his diary:

May the great God, whom I worship, grant to my Country and for the benefit of Europe in general, a great and glorious Victory: and may no misconduct, in any one, tarnish it: and may humanity after victory be the predominant feature in the British Fleet.

For myself individually, I commit my life to Him who made me and may His blessing light upon my endeavours for serving my Country faithfully.

To him I resign myself and the just cause which is entrusted to me to defend.

Amen. Amen. Amen.

Before the battle commenced he ordered for the famous signal to be raised: 'England expects every man to do his duty.' By four o'clock that afternoon Nelson was dead.

EVER THE OPTIMIST

It may look like a bathtub with a mast, but the Optimist dinghy forms the bedrock of worldwide sailing. Designer Clark Mills built the first Oppy (as they are affectionately known) in 1947. More than a quarter of a million have been built since and Optimists remain the most popular way for young people to get afloat. Oppies are sailed in over 110 countries by over 150,000 young people and it is the only dinghy approved by the International Sailing Federation exclusively for sailors under 16 years of age. Over 60% of the skippers at the 2004 Athens Olympics were former Optimist sailors and over 50% of the medal-winning skippers competed at Optimist International Championships.

WHAT TO DO IF YOU COME
ACROSS A MINE

1 Do not shoot at it. You may think that a shot from a rifle at a safe distance may set off the mine. However it's possible for the bullet to pierce the mine without triggering the detonator. The mine may then sink and be washed ashore in a dangerous state.

2 Do not try and tow it to port. Obvious, really.

3 Note the time and your position and report the sighting to the naval authorities via the Coastguard. Broadcast on Channel 16 so that other shipping in the vicinity is aware.

4 The Annual Summary of Admiralty Notices to Mariners contains information for fishermen who are unlucky enough to pick up a mine in their nets.

PERILS OF THE SEA

Huckleberry Finn and his friends were beginning to wish that they had stayed at home to paint the picket fence after all.

SONGS FOR SAILORS

Anchorage, Michelle Shocked
Dignity (A Ship Called), Deacon Blue
Driftwood, Travis
Ferry Cross the Mersey, Gerry and the Pacemakers
Fisherman's Dream, John Martyn
Fisherman's Song, Carly Simon
Friggin' in the Riggin', Sex Pistols
Love Boat, Kylie Minogue
Mermaids, Paul Weller
Queen of the Slipstream, Van Morrison
River Man, Nick Drake
Rudderless, Lemonheads
Sail Away, David Gray
Sail On, Commodores
Sailing, Rod Stewart
Sailor, Petula Clarke
Sailor to a Siren, Meat Loaf
Sailors Are Made to Travel, Edith Piaf
Seasick, Yet Still Docked, Morrissey
Ship to Shore, Chris de Burgh
Six Months in a Leaky Boat, Split Enz
The Tide is High, Blondie
Waves of Fear, Lou Reed

NAUTICAL PUZZLES

Which vice admiral might you find 50% of in a
square ring?
Answer on page 145

QUOTES ON BOATS

Raise your sail one foot and you get 10 feet of wind
Chinese proverb

ALONE IN AN OPEN BOAT

One of the greatest seafaring achievements, and one that went largely unnoticed, was the circumnavigation by a South African named Anthony Steward. Sailing around the world was nothing new, but what was remarkable is that he did it in an open boat.

NCS *Challenger* was 5.8m (19ft) long and had no cabin. There were waterproof lockers for clothes and food, but nowhere for Steward to escape the sun, wind and rain.

NCS *Challenger* had an open transom, meaning that the waves, which constantly broke over her, could drain freely off the back of the boat.

Capsizes were a routine occurrence for Steward, who was almost killed when his boat was struck by a cargo ship off South America. He was also dis-masted in the Pacific and shipwrecked for nine days in a remote corner of the Seychelles. His voyage around the world took 260 days.

A NAUTICAL JOKE

A young wife, her boorish husband and a young good-looking sailor were shipwrecked on an island.

One morning, the sailor climbed a tall coconut tree and yelled, 'Stop making love down there!'

'What's the matter with you?' the husband said when the sailor climbed down. 'We weren't making love.'

'Sorry,' said the sailor, 'From up there it looked like you were.'

Every morning thereafter, the sailor scaled the same tree and yelled the same thing. Finally the husband decided to climb the tree and see for himself.

With great difficulty, he made his way to the top. When he looked down, the husband said to himself, 'By golly he's right! It does look like they're making love down there!'

GOTCHA!

Yachting wit is tested on occasion by the yachting press and *Yachting Monthly* in particular. It's certainly not an annual occurrence, but the April issue of this venerable journal often contains a story that should be taken with a pinch of sea salt. News of a revolutionary floating anchor was met with astonishment by some, but wry smiles by the more astute. Sailors on the River Hamble were in uproar about plans for a Sail-thru McDonald's, as were yachtsmen in Jersey and Guernsey when informed that the bridge to be built between the two islands would curtail their cruising. Dogs that could sniff out wood-worm were considered a good thing, however, and it was hoped that they would also be able to detect the dreaded polyestermite that allegedly chews through fibreglass boats.

THE BIRTH OF THE OUTBOARD

Legend has it that the outboard engine was invented by American engineer Ole Evinrude in 1906 after he had almost fainted after rowing across Lake Okauchee in Wisconsin to fetch an ice cream for a lady friend. In fact Evinrude was not the first, although he is the only one of the pioneers whose name is still known. The way had been prepared for his success by men such as T Reece of Philadelphia, who patented a hand-driven screw propeller. Attached by screw clamps, it could be moved from boat to boat and in many ways was the forerunner of the modern outboard. Variations followed but it was a Frenchman, Trouvé, who claimed to have invented the first electric motorised outboard in 1888. In 1896 the American Motors Company produced a petrol-powered version and Evinrude's outboard followed a decade later. It could develop 1.5hp via its horizontal cylinder, vertical crankshaft and underwater gear housing. The rest is outboard history.

WHISKY, HOTEL, ALFA, TANGO?

Radio reception at sea can often be unclear, with yachts pitching on the waves and motor boats not having the advantage of a mast on which to put their aerial. Add the sound of the wind and engines, and it can become necessary to spell important words phonetically. There is an agreed vocabulary in order to prevent misunderstandings, as follows:

A	Alfa	J	Juliet	S	Sierra
B	Bravo	K	Kilo	T	Tango
C	Charlie	L	Lima	U	Uniform
D	Delta	M	Mike	V	Victor
E	Echo	N	November	W	Whisky
F	Foxtrot	O	Oscar	X	X-ray
G	Golf	P	Papa	Y	Yankee
H	Hotel	Q	Quebec	Z	Zulu
I	India	R	Romeo		

SAIL REPAIR KIT

Here's what you should have on board to cope with most emergencies:

Needles: smear with Vaseline and keep in an airtight container to prevent rust.

Palm: a leather cover for your thumb and palm that allows you to drive needles through thick sailcloth.

Sail slides: losing a slide is likely to cause further sail failure.

Sailcloth: assorted sizes and weights.

Sticky-back Dacron: can be used as a short-term repair.

Thread and twine: carry different weights and grades of sailmakers' thread and whipping twine.

Tools: scissors, pliers, hammer, grommets and punches, Stanley knife, lighter.

Webbing: to reinforce repairs. Tape: you can never have too much tape.

HOW TO GET KNOTTED

The sheet bend

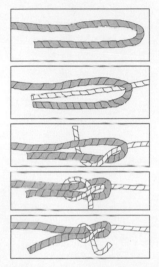

Take the end of two ropes and make a bight (open loop)
in the thicker rope. Pass the thinner rope through the
bight then around and under it. Loop the thinner rope
over the thicker part then under its own standing part.
Pull tight and check that loose ends are both on the
same side.

NAUTICAL PUZZLES

Where can you sail no lower yet float no higher?
Answer on page 145

DURING THE COMPILATION OF THIS BOOK, THE COMPANION TEAM...

Went sailing 47 times, and ran aground twice

Lost three wellies to the mud

Discovered the impenetrable world of nautical nomenclature

Resolved to pack in work, sell the house and sail to somewhere sunny twice daily

Thought to put on their oilies only after the skies had opened up on at least five occasions

Reminded themselves that a bad day afloat beats a good day in the office

Prepared and ate 36 ham and salad rolls, 14 of which were soggy

Spent 13 hours practising knots

Remembered leaky heads and fiddling about with impellers and forgot the plans to sail into the sunset

Wondered if there could be really be a need for quite so many knots

Compiled 89 jokes about seamen, 21 of which were of negligible comic value, and none of which were printable

Drank 270 cups of tea, of which 18 were made with UHT milk, and three of which were knocked over during accidental gybes

Imbibed 14 pints of Guinness at the London boat show

Abandoned ship

Please note that although every effort has been made to ensure accuracy in this book, the above statistics may be the result of waterlogged minds; take them with a pinch of salt.

NAUTICAL PUZZLES

The answers. As if you needed them.

P11 First, fill up the three-litre jug. Pour the three litres into the five-litre container. Refill the three-litre jug and once again pour it into the five-litre container until it is full. The three-litre jug now contains one litre. Empty the five-litre container back into the storage tank and then pour the one litre of diesel into it. Now, fill the three-litre jug up again and pour it into the yachtsman's five-litre container. The container will now contain the desired four litres.

P14 Clare Francis, who was sponsored by Robertsons Jam in the days when the company used the golliwog logo. Her yacht was named *Robertson's Golly*.

P17 112 – two sides will need 29 nails each, the other two sides only 27 nails each, as the nails in the corners double up.

P22 Your temper.

P46 You sail a lilac yacht with a keel from Denmark (probably). If you don't, you don't think like the rest of us.

P53 Pungy – the Pungy is a type of schooner from Chesapeake Bay, where it was used for dredging oysters. The others are canoes common to the Micronesian Islands and Malay Archipelago.

P58 Fill the sink and then let the water drain out. If the water circulates anticlockwise then you're in the Northern Hemisphere; if it goes out in a clockwise swirl then you're in the Southern Hemisphere.

P63 Man overboard.

P68 Two hours – 26 ÷ (7+6).

P78 Sixty-six feet. One half (three-sixths) is in the ground, one third (two-sixths) is underwater, which leaves one-sixth, which measures 11 feet. If one-sixth equals 11 feet, six-sixths equals 66 feet.

P100 All hands on deck.

P109 Women and children first.

P110 The seven seas.

P116 Either – any port in a storm!

P139 Vice Admiral Horatio Lord Nelson – the half-nelson is a wrestling hold in which the wrestler puts an arms under an opponent's arm and exerts pressure on the back of the neck.

P143 On the Dead Sea. It is lowest point on the Earth's surface, some 400m below actual sea level, yet its high salinity makes it incredibly buoyant.

SAILING NOTES, JOTTINGS, IDEAS AND DOODLES

SAILING NOTES, JOTTINGS, IDEAS AND DOODLES

SAILING NOTES, JOTTINGS, IDEAS AND DOODLES

SAILING NOTES, JOTTINGS, IDEAS AND DOODLES

SAILING NOTES, JOTTINGS, IDEAS AND DOODLES

SAILING NOTES, JOTTINGS, IDEAS AND DOODLES

SAILING NOTES, JOTTINGS, IDEAS AND DOODLES

SAILING NOTES, JOTTINGS, IDEAS AND DOODLES

SAILING NOTES, JOTTINGS, IDEAS AND DOODLES

SAILING NOTES, JOTTINGS, IDEAS AND DOODLES

SAILING NOTES, JOTTINGS, IDEAS AND DOODLES

SAILING NOTES, JOTTINGS, IDEAS AND DOODLES

SAILING NOTES, JOTTINGS, IDEAS AND DOODLES

SAILING NOTES, JOTTINGS,
IDEAS AND DOODLES

IT'S ALL BEEN PLAIN SAILING
BECAUSE OF...

my father and mother who gave me a love of the sea, and
my wife, who gave me a son to pass that love on to.

And thanks to
Judy Darley, Felicity Egerton, Selina Erham,
Nicola Haynes, Lois Lee, Nancy Waters